TEACH YOURSELF BOOKS

KARATE

Karate is undoubtedly the most effective form of self-defence. But it is also an exercise in physical and mental balance, and one of the toughest forms of physical training in existence. Because of the different systems developed by the major Karate schools, and the complexity of the movements and breathing, this book can only introduce the beginner to Karate. It covers a series of basic movements built up upon some of the basic postures and hopes to interest the reader sufficiently for him to want to join a club, where he will study the system in use by the club instructor.

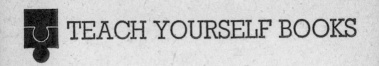
TEACH YOURSELF BOOKS

KARATE

Eric Dominy

Judo Black Belt Holder and British International
Co-founder of the London Karate Kai

Illustrated by
Peter Johnson

TEACH YOURSELF BOOKS
HODDER & STOUGHTON
ST PAUL'S HOUSE   WARWICK LANE   LONDON EC4P 4AH

First printed 1967
Eighth impression 1975

Copyright © 1967
The English Universities Press Ltd.

ISBN 0 340 05966 4

*Printed in Great Britain for Teach Yourself Books,
Hodder and Stoughton
by Hazell Watson & Viney Ltd,
Aylesbury, Bucks*

Contents

Preface

KARATE is an unusual activity in that the experts are not in full agreement upon its aims. Self-defence or sport? Exercise or philosophy?

The majority of its devotees are attracted by the self-defence movements upon which it is based, and there can be no doubt that Karate is the most effective form of self-defence. Karate is, however, far more than just this. It is an exercise in physical and mental balance, and one of the toughest forms of physical training in existence. It is also claimed that it moulds the personality of its exponents.

To make any form of self-defence effective only requires a comparatively small number of movements and practice until they become instinctive. Add to these movements a series of counter-attacks, and you have a crude and basic form of Karate—crude but effective. However, a display of this form of self-defence and counter-attack would horrify the genuine Karateman.

What, then, is Karate? Basically, it is a series of self-defence and counter-attack tactics based on traditional movements. These are run into formal series, called "Katas" in Japanese, and they are taught and practised without change year after year. At one time, there were hundreds of Karate Schools in Japan, each with its own Katas; but at the present time they have been reduced to just a few associations, each teaching its own system to its own affiliated clubs. The system of each school or association has its own merits and failings, and I think that the unswerving belief in the perfection of the systems of one's own school tends to delay progress. There is a tendency to retain movements and postures because they are traditional to the school, rather than because they are effective.

Many are the stories told about the beginnings of Karate, and the exploits of its heroes, but the tales of its development are mainly fictitious, and although they are well worth reading as Mediaeval and Oriental James Bond stories, not too much attention should be paid to them. Wherever Karate started, there is no doubt that it was in Japan that it developed and was brought to the present stage of perfection.

The genuine Karate exponent demands much more than the automatic performance of Kata. He aims at rhythm and perfection, and beauty of movement. This he regards as far more vital than the effectiveness of the defence and counter-attack. In addition, to utilise the full power of his body, the pupil is expected to develop complete control over his breathing. Correct breathing greatly increases the effectiveness of his movement and balance. This, of course, applies to other sports, such as weightlifting and swimming.

At a good school, the pupil is taught that Karate was designed for protection, and was never intended to be used for attack. A Karateman never hurts anyone unless he is attacked first.

The main requirements are technique, speed, and strength, but when training for one it is essential that the others should not be overlooked or neglected. The cost of learning varies from school to school. Naturally, a fee is charged for instruction, and most schools require their pupils to wear the regulation clothing, consisting of light, white trousers and jacket, as shown in the illustrations in this book. Certainly it is possible to perform Karate whilst wearing old trousers and a sweater, but this is untidy and the clothing not easy to keep clean. Personally, I think pupils should wear regulation clothing, and keep it clean at all times. Most schools supply the clothing, or can put their pupils in touch with a supplier.

Because of the different systems developed by the major schools, and the complexity of the movements and breathing, a book of this size can only introduce the reader to Karate. Several volumes would be required to cover the techniques and Katas used by each school; therefore I have only attempted to cover the outlines.

After considerable research and discussion, I have decided to cover a series of basic movements built up upon some of the Basic Postures. This will introduce the reader to Karate and, I hope, interest him sufficiently to make him join a club. At this stage, he will study the system in use by the club instructor.

Japanese terms are used almost exclusively in Karate schools and clubs. However, they tend to vary in different schools, and each Kata has its own Japanese name. For this reason I have avoided the use of technical terms in this book. It is little use a reader devoting time to learning names or movements if he has to learn a fresh series when he joins a club. I have given each movement its English name, and I am sure that this will enable the reader to follow my description without difficulty.

Karate is not dangerous to the beginner. In the advanced stages of free-fighting and contest, knocks and bruises may be expected, but the beginner need have no fear if care is taken. However, some of the defensive movements, if carried out with a little too much enthusiasm, can throw the attacker onto his back. For this reason, and because of the emphasis placed upon posture and balance, I always advise pupils to take a Judo "Beginners' Course" first. It can do no harm, and a knowledge of the methods of falling—which is seldom included in a Karate syllabus—is very useful.

Only a few years ago, Karate was unknown in Britain, but now few large towns are without a club or school. Should a reader be unable to trace his local club, I shall be pleased to assist anyone who writes to me, enclosing a stamped, addressed envelope.

I wish to thank Jeff Smallcombe of London Judo Society for his help in the preparation of the photographs from which the drawings for this book were made. Also my thanks to Peter Johnson, who took the photographs and drew all the illustrations.

ERIC DOMINY

London Judo Society and Karate Kai,
  32 St. Oswold's Place,
    London, S.E.11

1. About Karate

IT is extremely difficult to define Karate. It is linked in the public mind with Judo but no doubt this is because both developed in Japan and both are practised in similar garments. In fact the Karate jacket, not having to take much strain from pulling and tugging, is much lighter in weight but this is not obvious on a casual inspection. In both, participants work in bare feet.

Not so long ago Judo men, on attaining the distinction of black belt, were introduced to atemi which is the art of disabling opponents by striking at nerve centres and other vital parts of the body. Karate is a further development of this form of fighting. It is said that Karate developed when the Japanese, having overrun the Luchu Islands, refused to allow the Islanders to carry weapons. As a result Karate was devised as the only form of self-defence available to them.

More recently, like Judo, the word "do" meaning "way" was added. This was intended to indicate that Karate-do had an ethical basis and was not just a form of aggression or self-defence. The present-day Karatemen insist that whilst their art is a most effective form of self-defence, this is only in addition to its value as a form of physical and mental training. Karate, like Judo, has developed a philosophy of its own. What proportion philosophy bears to practical work varies greatly from school to school. Some schools emphasise the practical to such an extent that they judge their success and like to be judged by the public progress their pupils make in smashing wood and tiles. Astounded spectators can see this sort of progress for themselves, but history does not relate how many pupils suffer from painfully broken

9

hands later in life. At the other extreme are the teachers who believe that the most important side of Karate is the beauty of the techniques and the rhythm and poetry of the sequences of movements. In addition we have to take into account the shouts which are given out by the attacker as he strikes and the defender as he wards-off. These shouts have great significance in Karate. They are brought out from the stomach and are said to—and do—strengthen the body as they are made. These shouts are outside the scope of this book as they require long and personal instruction from a first-class teacher. Meanwhile the blows and kicks included in this book are sufficiently powerful for all practical self-defence.

There is no doubt that a trained Karateman can smash boards, tiles and bricks with his bare hands, elbows, feet and head, but this is a side many experts prefer to hide away from publicity. It should be remembered that the reader of this book may well find himself able to perform some of these tricks but unless he is extremely well taught he is likely to do himself permanent and painful injury. Personal and prolonged instruction is required before this stage is reached.

Karate is taught in the form of a series of katas. These are series of formal exercises in which the basic movements are practised. There are very many different katas and these vary from school to school.

There is however a form of Karate in which free-fighting takes place. In this, punches—and kicks—are pulled at the last second and the exponents are expected to call out admitting defeat when a blow would have landed had the fight been serious.

As a form of defence Karate has several advantages over other methods. Anyone of any age can practise it and practise it alone and no special equipment is required. With reasonable precautions there is no danger, and finally no great exertion is required.

Whilst reasonable proficiency can be attained from written instruction, to attain a really high standard it is necessary to obtain expert instruction. In Britain at the moment such instruction is very rare but European

Instructors are now returning from Japan, where many have studied for several years, to provide a cadre of teachers in whom the pupil may place complete confidence.

Karate means "empty hand" and all attacks are made with no more than the weapons provided by nature. These are the hand, foot, elbow, head and knee. It is important to use these weapons correctly as failure to do so will not only reduce the effect of the blow but may cause painful injury to the Karateman. An obvious example is a punch. If it is delivered with the thumb tucked inside the fingers a hard punch will result in a broken thumb. If the thumb is left outside there is less danger of injury.

The Weapons Used in Karate

The Clenched Fist

The fingers are clenched tightly with the thumb wrapped round the fore and middle fingers. The blow is delivered with the root joints of the fore and middle fingers (Fig. 1) or

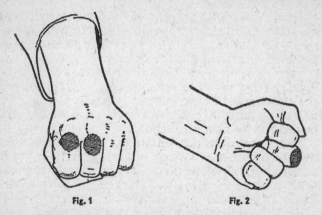

Fig. 1   Fig. 2

the projecting knuckle of the middle finger (Fig. 2). The target is usually the opponent's face or the softer parts of his body.

The Half-Clenched Fist

In this method the fingers are bent back at the middle joint only, the thumb pressing down on the forefinger. In this manner the blow can be delivered with the

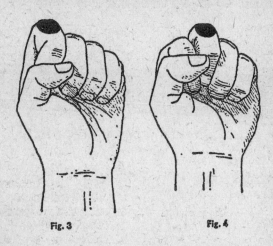

Fig. 3   Fig. 4

knuckle of the forefinger (Fig. 3) or middle finger (Fig. 4), the root joint of the middle finger (Fig. 5). Again the face is the usual target.

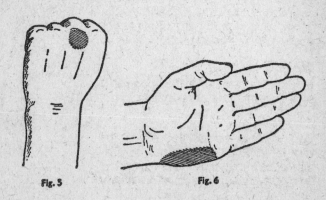

Fig. 5   Fig. 6

The Straight Hand

The four fingers are kept close together and extended. The fingers are then used for thrusting at parts of the body such as the eyes or solar-plexus. The edge of the hand can also be used for striking or chopping (Fig. 6).

The Two Finger Hand

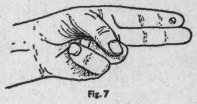

Fig. 7

In this case the little finger and adjoining finger are bent as is the thumb. The fore and middle fingers being extended for thrusting, usually at the opponent's eyes (Fig. 7).

Single Finger Hand

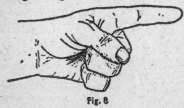

Fig. 8

Only the forefinger is outstretched, the other fingers and thumb being bent (Fig. 8). The target in this case is the eye.

Base of the Hand

With the finger and thumb together and outstretched, the heel of the palm of the hand is used for pushing at the opponent's face, chest, etc. (Fig. 9).

The Elbow

Mainly used to attack the opponent's solar-plexus, chest or abdomen.

Base of the Toes

The toes are turned upward as the kick is delivered. A mistimed or misplaced kick can cause damage to the toes or ankles so care must be taken.

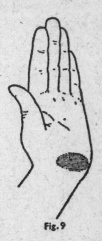

Fig. 9

The kick is delivered forward to the opponent's body. When shoes are worn, obviously the toes cannot be turned up and the toe of the shoe is used.

The Heel

This is used for a rear or downward kick. The opportunity would arise if you were held from the rear. The kick could then be delivered to the opponent's instep, groin, knee or shin.

Side of Foot

The toes are turned upward and the little toe edge of the foot is used sideways. The attack is used against the knee or other joint. A mistake can seriously damage the toes. The technique is similar to the more familiar blow delivered with the side of the hand.

Knee Cap

Used to attack the groin, stomach or head.

Head

To the opponent's face with the forehead just below the hair-line, much as heading a football. The top of the head may also be used against the stomach.

Hammer-Fist

The little finger side of the clenched fist is brought down

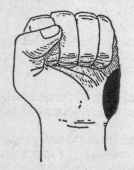

Fig. 10

on the opponent's head or temple as one would use a hammer (Fig. 10).

Warding-off and Defence

Karate is a form of self-defence. This means of course that the Karateman is attacked and cannot count on getting in the first blow. As there is no point in learning Karate only to be laid out by an attacker's first blow, it is essential to have the ability to ward-off attacks made against you. Carried out correctly this not only provides a successful defence but also opens up the opponent to your Karate counters.

Most attacks can be warded-off with the forearm. Naturally the soft inner side should never be used as this leaves the arteries open to injury. Instead the sharp edges of the forearm are brought into action. These are the inner or thumb side edge, the outer or little finger side edge and occasionally the back of the forearm. These are shown in Fig. 11. It will be found that by warding the attacker's arm away (outwards) his body is automatically left open to the counter. In Fig. 12 the defender on the left is blocking the attack and opening up his opponent for the counter-blow shown in Fig. 13.

Fig. 11

Immediately you have warded-off a blow or delivered one of your own, your arm should be withdrawn. Unless you do this you are, in your turn, leaving yourself open to counter.

The ball or edge of the foot can be used for countering kicks delivered against you. This will be described later in the book.

It is important that even defensive movements should be made constructively. Whilst to push the opponent's arm away when he strikes at you may be effective in that it prevents the blow landing, it does nothing to stop a second attempt being made. If instead, the blow is deflected with a powerful chopping action so delivered that the sharp edge of the forearm makes contact with

Fig. 12   Fig. 13

the soft underside of the attacker's forearm the result is decisive and extremely painful. The attacker's arm is put out of action and not only is a second attempt ruled out but he is unlikely to be able to defend himself against your counter-action.

All defensive action should be made against one of the vulnerable points on the opponent's body with one of the natural counter-attacking weapons already described in this chapter.

Vital Spots of the Body and Methods of Attack

The charts published by the Japanese Karate Associations list a large number of vital points which may be attacked. Blows delivered to some of the points can kill, others cause no more than pain, but all when struck correctly will cause at least intense pain and for this reason Karate should be used against an opponent with the greatest care except when defending against an unlawful attack which is delivered with the intention of causing you injury.

Many of the vital points of the body are shown in Figs. 14 and 15. Some of the methods of attack are as follows:

1. Crown of the head — Fist or edge of hand
2. Between crown of head and forehead — Fist and edge of hand
3. Temple — Fist, edge of hand and four finger hand
4. The ears — Fist, edge of hand or four finger hand
5. Between the eyes — Fist, edge of hand, fingertips, etc.
6. Above and below the eyes — Fist, edge of hand, fingertips, etc.
7. The eyes — Knuckles or fingertips
8. Just below the nose — Fist, edge of hand, fingertips, knuckles

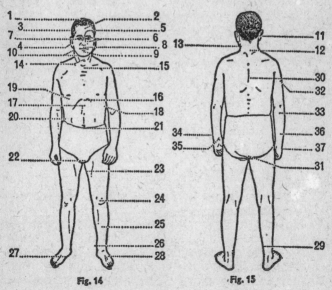

Fig. 14   Fig. 15

9. Just below lower lip	Fist, edge of hand, fingertips, knuckles
10. The jaw	Fist, foot, elbow
11. Behind the ears	Fist, fingertips, edge of hand
12. Back of neck	Fist, edge of hand, knuckles, elbow, foot
13. Side of neck	Fist, edge of hand, knuckles, elbow, foot
14. Throat	Fist, fingertips, knuckles, knee, elbow, foot
15. Top of breastbone	Fist, knee, elbow, foot
16. Base of breastbone	Fist, knee, elbow, foot
17. Solar-plexus	Fist, knee, elbow, foot
18. Side of body just below armpits	Fist, knee, kick, elbow
19. Just below nipples	Fist, knee, kick, elbow
20. Side of body just above hips	Fist, knee, kick, elbow
21. Just below navel	Fist, knee, kick, elbow
22. Testicles	Fist, knee, kick, elbow, edge of hand
23. Inside of upper thigh	Kick or fist
24. Knee	Kick, knee, elbow
25. Shinbone	Fist, knee, elbow, kick
26. Ankle	Kick, knee, elbow, fist
27. Top of foot	Kick, knee, heel
28. Instep	Heel, kick
29. Back of leg just above the ankle	Kick, fist, elbow
30. Between the shoulder blades	Kick, fist, elbow, knee
31. Base of spine	Kick, knee, elbow, fist
32. Upper part of the back of the arm	Edge of hand, fist, elbow
33. Elbow	Fist, knee, elbow, kick
34. Wrist	Edge of hand, fist, elbow
35. Inside wrist (pulse)	Edge of hand, fist
36. Back of forearm	Fist, knee, kick
37. Back of the hand	Edge of the hand, fist

This list is by no means complete. I have restricted the parts of the body shown to those which are easily located. Many of the vital points shown on comprehensive charts would require an expert to locate them.

Similarly I have not attempted to complete the list of the natural weapons which can be used to attack each vital spot. A little experiment on yourself will soon reveal just how vulnerable each point really is to attack. For example, you will find that whilst to attack the wrist with the edge of the hand may well disable the opponent, a similar attack to his head would be more likely to disable you.

For the same reason I have not included every possible attack against each vulnerable point. For an attack to the crown of the head I have shown the fist or edge of the hand. If, however, the attacker bends himself sufficiently for you to use your elbow, naturally you would do so. Equally, you would use the heel or knee to other points if the opponent was on the ground or you could reach them for some other reason. You must use intelligence just as much as knowledge.

Finally, it must be remembered that it is essential to withdraw the foot, arm, etc., immediately your blow has been attempted. Failure to do this leaves you off balance and gives the initiative to the opponent. In addition, by withdrawing the hand or foot to the basic position which will be described, you will be ready to deal with a second attack. As a rule the ward-off is made with one hand, arm or foot, whilst the counter-attack is made with the other.

2. Practice and Training

IN many books on Karate you read of experts practising by striking at hard surfaces, such as boards, hundreds of times a day. This is done to harden the edges of the hands, feet and other natural weapons. I have seen leading Japanese experts in action breaking bricks and large stones and I am sure such training is effective *for experts*. Should the casual reader of a book attempt the same thing he is only likely to damage his hands or feet and may cause himself pain for life. In addition remember that blows to certain vital spots, made by even an untaught person, may kill.

For these reasons I do not advise the setting up of an elaborate training apparatus. Every movement can be practised before a large mirror and on a dummy no harder than a boxing punch bag. As most people do not have such an item in their garden shed, a good substitute is an army kit-bag, which can be purchased for a few shillings, filled with old rags and newspaper.

Remember that no matter how hard or often you practise, it is an entirely different matter when you are faced with not a bag full of paper but a vicious opponent who is attempting to push your face in with a bottle. The best defence is always to avoid getting yourself into a situation in which self-defence is required. If you do meet such a situation despite my warning then remember the old adage:

> "If defend yourself you must
> Learn Judo or Karate first."

Once you have really got an idea of the postures and movements you must find a partner in order to practise the techniques on a moving person and in the actual situations which might arise. Finally, it is possible to practise free-fighting. Even better, instead of finding a partner, join a good club. Clubs in Britain are very few indeed and in many cases this will be impossible. However, it should be possible to spend a few days on a course or to visit a club just to get the idea. Whilst the principles remain the same, the details of the techniques and forms of teaching vary considerably from school to school, but do not let this discourage you. If the club instructor's methods vary from those in this book, use his. Practical instruction is always far better than theoretical teaching from a book, however good the book may be.

In Judo the throws and ground holds and locks can be taught and practised by actually performing the technique. This is impossible in Karate as the landing of a blow may cause severe pain. Karate movements therefore have to be practised by checking the blows just before they reach their target. To simulate the real thing, series of katas, or formal exercises have been developed, each association having its own. By means of these the student can, with a little imagination, visualise an opponent and keep his movement and interest flowing. In this book I have developed series of similar movements or sequences of movements rather than follow any particular form of kata. From these series the reader should have no difficulty in adapting to the particular katas of any club he may join.

3. Basic Posture and Movement

The Basic Posture

The student adopts the Basic Posture. His body is upright with his feet placed about shoulder-width apart. His arms hang relaxed with his hands lightly clenched in front of him, one either side of the knot of his belt (Fig. 16):

Fig. 16   Fig. 17   Fig. 18

A Second Basic Posture

There is a second Basic Posture which is used when protecting the upper part of the body and making counter-attacks to the upper part of the attacker's body. In this case the arms are bent at the elbows, the fists being held level with the shoulders, palms of the hands facing the shoulders (Fig. 17). Having warded-off a blow to the head with, say, the left arm, there is no need to take the fist back to the basic position at the hip. Instead it can be taken back to the shoulder.

This alternative posture, of course, leads us into a second series of defences and counter-attacks. Another book would be required to describe these, but an interested reader can develop and incorporate many of these for himself.

When adopting the position shown in Fig. 17, do not hold the fists too close to the shoulders. A little experiment will show you that it is possible to make a far more rapid counter-punch if the fists are held some twelve inches in front of the shoulders than when they are held very close to them.

Attack 1

Movement 1

From the Basic Posture advance your left foot and arm, at the same time taking your right arm back a little. This position is shown in Fig. 18 and is, in effect, the sort of defensive posture you would expect to adopt against an attack with the right leg or hand. Your left, defensive, arm is held forward, the arm almost parallel with the left thigh but about 18 to 24 inches above it, as convenient and comfortable. The left side of the body is now facing the imaginary opponent, with the eyes watching his face. The left hand is lightly clenched. Your right arm is bent at the elbow at a little more than 90° with the hand open or lightly clenched, ready to attack. Note how the toes are turned outwards and the trunk is held upright. The posture is strong and well balanced. As in a Judo attack, the hips have been lowered by bending the knee, in this case the left, and the lower abdomen has been made strong. Resume the Basic Posture.

Movement 2

Your right foot and leg are advanced, the left fist being taken back against the left hip (Fig. 19). This is a fast dynamic movement; the leg and both arms moving at the same speed. Should your left arm move more slowly than the right you will lose balance and, in addition, should the opponent evade your blow, you will be weak defensively. On the other hand, should the right hand move slowly there will be insufficient power to your attack. The right

Fig. 19   Fig. 20

foot is advanced along the ground in a gliding movement. If you experiment you will find that raising the leg results in the arc of the blow of your fist being deflected and weakened. Do not overstride with your leg as this will again weaken the blow and cause you to lose balance. The right forearm is turned so that the back of the hand is upwards. The wrist is absolutely straight and the fist, wrist, forearm and upper-arm are in a straight line from your shoulder. The blow is aimed at the chest or middle of the opponent's body.

The left fist is placed at your hip, loosely clenched, where it is ready to deal with any counter-attack by warding-off or catching a blow.

It is important that the shoulders should be kept down. To raise the shoulders, as if shrugging them, weakens the posture and greatly reduces the effect of the blow.

The trunk is again kept upright, the eyes looking into the eyes of your imaginary opponent.

These points apply throughout this book, although in the interests of brevity I have not always repeated them each time this type of movement is made. Therefore, repeat the movements time after time.

Attack 2

Movement 1

From the Basic Posture the left leg and arm are advanced, the right hand being taken back and down to the right hip. The action is, of course, exactly the same as that described in Attack 1, but this time a left-hand blow is delivered and the right hand and arm take up the defensive role.

Movement 2

The right leg and arm are moved forward, the left hand moving back to the hip. The movement must be dynamic, both arms and the leg moving at the same speed, the leg reaching the ground shortly before the arm reaches the conclusion of its movement as it has less far to travel.

This series of movements can be repeated as many times as your stamina and the time available will allow. Repeated punches will however tend to stretch the muscles and joints of the arms with the result that you can develop a painful elbow similar to tennis elbow. Because of this I advise care and reasonably short sessions at first.

Attack 3

Movement 1

Again adopt the Basic Posture (Fig. 16), but this time, as you take your left foot forward you drive forward your right fist and leave your left hand, lightly clenched,

K.—2

in the vicinity of your left hip. (See Fig. 20.) Advance
your left foot and drive forward with your left arm,
bringing your right fist down to your right hip. This is
called the Reverse Movement as, instead of using the
natural movement of left leg and opposite arm, the
corresponding leg and arm are advanced together.

Again note the straight back and upright head, your
eyes gazing into the eyes of the imaginary opponent.

Movement 2

The position is changed, the right foot and arm driving
forward and the left fist going back to a defensive posture
on the left hip.

The two movements are repeated time after time.

Attack 4

Movement 1

This is similar to Attack 1. Made from the Basic Posture,
but instead of attacking the middle of the opponent's
body this time your blow is aimed at his face. The blow
should be aimed at targets such as his forehead, eyes or the
vital spot beneath his nose. You might use the fingers or
the fist with one or two knuckles advanced to make
contact.

From your basic position advance your left foot and
arm, moving the arm so that the blow is aimed at the
opponent's face. The right hand comes down to the right
hip.

Movement 2

The right fist and leg drive forward, the left fist coming
back to the left hip. As in all the movements just described, the attacking arm is held so that the back of the
hand is upward, the wrist and forearm being completely
straight (Fig. 19). The head is upright and the trunk kept
straight.

Attack 5

Movement 1

The same principles apply, but this time you are countering a kick or punch to the body. From the Basic Posture advance your left leg and arm, the right fist coming down to the right hip. Your left arm thrusts downwards and to your front to catch the opponent's right arm or leg as he attacks your body. In this Karate movement it is the custom to catch the opponent's shin or forearm and push it downwards, but having been brought up in Judo, I consider this to be inefficient and dangerous to the fingers and thumb. I much prefer to ward-off the attack with the fist or an outward chopping movement of the little finger edge of the forearm. This movement allows more room for possible misjudgement and can, if well directed, disable the opponent's arm or leg.

Movement 2

As the attack is turned away take the right leg and arm forward, driving your fist downward to your opponent's solar-plexus, abdomen or groin as convenient.

Note: Naturally you may not find your opponent directly in front of you when you have warded-off his attack, or you may have to deal with a second attack. In this case, as you drive your arm and leg forward in your counter-attack, turn in the required direction by pivoting on your rear foot. You will turn without difficulty or loss of concentration. The thrust always comes from the rear foot.

Attack 6

Movement 1

This defence is originated by stepping to your rear, and is called a rear-step defence. From the Basic Posture you take your right leg back, driving the left fist forward at the same time. Your right fist comes down to your right hip. This first movement is likely to be that used to block an opponent's blow.

Movement 2

The second movement is similar to those already practised, the right fist driving forward as the right leg moves in the same direction, and the left fist coming down to the left hip.

Continuation Movements

You can either start again from the Basic Posture by taking the step to the rear or alternatively make a third movement punching forward with the left fist and so on.

Attack 7

This is a complicated movement to describe, requiring as it does the use of both arms in quick succession. It is a ward-off and counter-attack with the little finger cutting edges of the hands. The imaginary opponent attacks with fist or foot to your body at about stomach level.

Movement 1

From the Basic Posture you take back your right foot, your right arm being raised across your chest and your left held in front of you. Both arms are bent at the elbow

Fig. 21

Fig. 22

with the hands so turned that the little finger edges are pointed downwards. In effect the arms are bent in much the same way as a whip is coiled ready to strike (Figs. 21 and 22).

Movement 2

You make a sweeping drive downwards and outwards with your left hand thrusting away an imaginary attack. The little finger edge of the left hand and forearm is used to ward-off, the hard bony side contacting the soft inside of the attacker's right leg or arm. The target is one of the vital points described in Chapter 1.

Movement 3

Step forward with the right foot, at the same time whipping the right forearm down and outwards to deliver a crippling counter-blow. The counter is aimed at one of the vital points. Although I have described the sweep of the arm as downwards it can be made upwards especially when the target is the neck, throat or face. The little finger cutting edge is the weapon used.

Attack 8

The attacker aims his attack at the upper part of your body. That is to say his target is your shoulders, neck or head.

Movement 1

From the Basic Posture step back with your right foot, sweeping your left arm, fist clenched, upwards and outwards to ward-off the attack. The right fist is placed by your right hip (Fig. 23). The ward-off is made with the little finger side of the fist and forearm.

Movement 2

Step forward with your right leg, driving your right fist upwards and forwards.

The target for your counter is your opponent's head, face or throat. As you drive forward with your right fist your left is brought back to your left hip at exactly the same speed.

Fig. 23   Fig. 24

Attack 9

This is a defence and counter to an attack aimed at the upper part of your body.

Movement 1

From the Basic Posture step back with your right foot bringing up your left arm, fist clenched, to ward-off the attack. Your right fist is at your right hip. Your left fist is turned so that the little finger edge is turned upwards.

Movement 2

Step forward with your right foot, bring up your right fist and then drive it downwards, little finger edge leading, to your opponent's head or face. The left fist is brought back to the left hip at the same speed.

Attack 10

Now we come to kicks. It must be remembered that kicks can be warded-off or the leg caught, so it is essential that

the Karateman delivers his kick at lightning speed
without sacrificing his balance. Just like the blow from
the fist the foot must be withdrawn fast whether or not
the kick has landed.

Movement 1

Adopt the Basic Posture (Fig. 16) with your fists close to
your hips, one on either side of the knot of your belt.
Now glide forward with the left leg (Fig. 24).

Movement 2

Keeping your fists at your hips, kick forward and upwards with your right leg. The contact with the opponent
is made with the ball of the foot. As you kick the left knee
is bent to improve your balance and although you kick as
far forward and upward as you can, you must keep your
trunk upright to preserve your balance (Fig. 25). To
conclude the movement bring the foot down and resume
the Basic Posture. Do not raise on the ball of the foot
upon which you are standing or this may cause you to
fall backwards.

Now kick with the other foot.

Attack 11

This is a kick to the side (that is to your right or left)
delivered with the little toe edge of the foot.

Movement 1

From the Basic Posture bend your left knee slightly for
balance and kick outwards to the right with the right
foot. The right leg is kept straight, the inside edge of the
foot being aimed at the opponent's knee or shin. Always
kick as high as you possibly can, but your trunk must be
kept upright and your fists at your hips (Fig. 26).

Movement 2

Repeat the kick, this time using the left foot.

Fig. 25   Fig. 26

Attack 12

This attack is delivered with the big toe edge of the foot. Because this movement involves crossing the feet, in my opinion a basic error, and the kick has not very much range, I do not consider it a very effective attack.

Movement 1

From the Basic Posture balance on your left leg, bending the knee slightly, and kick across your left leg at an opponent at your left side. The kick is aimed at his knee or shin. Your fists are kept at your hips and your trunk upright (Fig. 27).

Movement 2

Repeat the kick to your right with your left foot.

Notes: 1. During instruction Karate is practised in bare feet and there will be a real danger of damaging the feet if the

Fig. 27

kicks are made against a wall or other hard surface. In self-defence in the street, of course, you would be wearing shoes and no such danger would exist.

2. How to teach Karate has always been a problem. In many schools outside Japan where first-class experienced instructors are available it is the custom to strike at boards and other hard surfaces. This, I repeat, is bad, as it can lead to painful and permanent injury to the hand and foot. I have said that before, but it cannot be repeated too often. With experience it was found that the most effective method of teaching was by means of kata, or a balanced series of movements. The pupil repeats each movement time after time until each one can be performed accurately and smoothly. The repetition is very important indeed as it is the only way in which the pupil can achieve rhythm and effectiveness. A rhythmic, graceful movement is not only a pleasure to perform and watch but it is also far more effective than an ugly, ill-timed effort.

4. Further Basic Movements

Attack 1

Movement 1

Adopt the Basic Posture.

Take a longish gliding step forward with the right foot, at the same time punching forward with the right fist. The left fist remains at the left hip. This is of course a very basic movement. The blow is aimed at the opponent's chest. The trunk is kept upright and the right shoulder is not thrust forward as you punch (Fig. 28).

Return to the Basic Posture by withdrawing the right foot.

Movement 2

Step forward with the left foot, punching with the left fist. The right fist being taken to the right hip. The position is as shown in Fig. 28 but with left and right reversed throughout. Take the left foot and leg back to regain the Basic Posture.

Fig. 28

Attack 2

Movement 1

From the Basic Posture step forward with your right foot, punching at the opponent's face with your right fist. The left hand remains at the left hip. The trunk is kept upright and the right shoulder not advanced. The position is

illustrated in Fig. 28 but the punch is aimed higher.
Take the right foot and leg back, returning to the Basic
Posture.

Movement 2

Punch to the head with the left fist, stepping forward with
the left foot. The right hand moves to the right hip. Step
back to regain the Basic Posture.

Attack 3

This is an "opposition" movement in which the right
arm and left leg move together as you attack.

Movement 1

From the Basic Posture move your left foot forward
leaving the left fist at the hip and at the same time punching with the right fist to the opponent's chest. The trunk
is kept upright and the right shoulder not advanced.
Take back the left foot and bring down your right arm
to regain the Basic Posture.

Movement 2

Advance the right foot punching at the opponent's chest
with the left fist. The right fist goes to your right hip.
Withdraw the right leg and left fist to resume the Basic
Posture.

Attack 4

Movement 1

Advance the left leg and punch with the right fist to the
opponent's face. The left fist is taken to the left hip.
As usual the trunk is kept upright and faces the front,
the shoulder not being advanced as the punch is delivered.
Step back and lower the fists to return to the Basic
Posture.

Movement 2

Step forward with the right leg punching to the opponent's
face with the left fist, reversing all the movements made

in "Movement 1." Step back to return to the Basic Posture.

Attack 5

This is a combined ward-off and counter-blow. I have described it in two movements but it is obvious that the practised Karateman would make both the movements together to save time and thus gain in effectiveness.

Movement 1

From the Basic Posture step back with your right foot and taking your left fist up to your right shoulder sweep downwards and outwards across your body in order to dash away a kick or punch aimed at your stomach or groin. Contact is made with the little finger edge of your fist and forearm. This ward-off is a form of hammer-fist blow or a chop with the edge of the hand to the opponent's leg or arm.

Movement 2

Without moving your feet withdraw your left fist to your hip and punch with your right arm to your opponent's chest or stomach. Bring your left leg back to regain the Basic Posture.

Movement 3

Step forward with your right foot taking your right fist to your left shoulder and then sweeping outwards and downwards to ward-off an imaginary attack using the little finger edge of your right forearm and fist.

Movement 4

Taking your right fist back to your right hip, punch with your left fist at your opponent's chest or stomach without moving your feet. Finally, step back with your right foot to regain the Basic Posture.

Attack 6

This is a defence and counter to a punch delivered to your chest. It commences from the Basic Posture.

Movement 1

As the imaginary opponent punches with his right hand step back with your right foot leaving the right fist at your hip and taking your left fist up to your right shoulder sweep outwards and upwards with your left fist and forearm. Contact is made with the little finger edge so that the palm of the hand is held downwards.

Movement 2

Without moving your feet take your left fist back to your left hip at the same time drive your right fist to the opponent's stomach or chest. Take your left leg back to resume the Basic Posture.

Movement 3

Step back with your left foot taking your right fist to your left shoulder and then sweeping outwards and upwards with it to ward-off a punch with an opponent's left fist. Your left fist remains at your hip.

Movement 4

Returning your right fist to your hip drive forward with your left fist at the same time aiming at the opponent's chest or stomach. Take your right leg back to recover the Basic Posture.

Attack 7

This is a defence followed by a finger thrust as the counter. Your opponent punches at your chest or face with his right hand.

Movement 1

Step back with your right foot and take your left fist to your right shoulder, from there sweeping outwards and upwards to ward-off the attack with the little finger edge of the hand (the fist is clenched) and forearm.

Movement 2

Without moving your feet take your left hand back to your hip at the same time thrusting with your fingertip to the opponent's throat or other suitable vulnerable point with your right hand. Step back to the Basic Posture.

Movement 3

Step back with your left foot and taking your right fist across to your left shoulder ward-off outwards and upwards with a straight hand, little finger edge leading.

Movement 4

Returning your right fist to your hip drive your left fingertip to your opponent's throat or other vulnerable point within reach. Step back with your right leg to regain the Basic Posture.

Attack 8

In this attack you ward-off a right-handed attack to your eyes.

Movement 1

Take back your right foot leaving your right fist at your right hip. Your left arm sweeps upwards and outwards, little finger edge leading, warding-off the thrust to your eyes. The fingers of your left hand are outstretched to add length to your defence or you can use a hammer-fist blow (Fig. 29).

Movement 2

Without moving your feet bring your left fist back to your left hip at the same time drive your right fist upwards to your opponent's chest or face. Withdraw your left foot and bring your fists to the hip position to resume the Basic Posture.

Movement 3

To ward-off a left-handed blow to the eyes take back your left foot sweeping your right arm up and outwards, making contact with the little finger edge. Your left hand is retained close to the hip.

Movement 4

Take your right hand back to your hip at the same time punching upwards with your left fist to the opponent's chest or face. Withdraw your right foot and bring your left fist down to resume the Basic Posture.

Fig. 29   Fig. 30

Attack 9

This is a defence against an imaginary right-hand blow aimed downwards at your head.

Movement 1

Taking your right foot back sweep your left fist upwards so that the fist is at least slightly higher than your head (Fig. 30). The imaginary opponent's right-hand blow is swept away with the little finger edge of your forearm. The trunk is kept upright. Your right fist is retained at the hip.

Movement 2

Keeping your feet in the same position bring your left fist down to your left hip at the same time driving your right fist into the stomach of the opponent. Return to the Basic Posture.

Movement 3

Take your left foot back sweeping the right fist upwards
and outwards to ward-off a blow to the head made with
the opponent's left fist. Your left fist remains at the left
hip. The upward defensive sweep is made with the little
finger edge of the hand and forearm.

Movement 4

Without moving the feet the right hand is brought down
to the hip; at the same time the left fist is crashed into the
stomach of the imaginary opponent. The Basic Posture
is then resumed.

Attack 10

Defence and counter to a right-handed blow to the
stomach.

Movement 1

Take your right foot back keeping your right fist at the
hip at the same time raising your left fist upward and
forward. The little finger edge of the hand is upwards.

Movement 2

From this position your left fist is swept downwards and
outwards thus warding-off a blow to your stomach.

Movement 3

The right fist is driven to the opponent's stomach, the
left being taken to the left hip. The feet are not moved.
Return to the Basic Posture.

Attack 11

Defence and counter to a left-handed blow to the
stomach.

Movement 1

Take back your left foot raising the right fist over to

shoulder level in front of you. The left fist is held at the hip.

Movement 2
Sweep the right fist downwards and outwards driving an imaginary blow to your stomach away from you.

Movement 3
Drive the left fist to the opponent's stomach, taking the right back to the hip. Resume the Basic Posture.

Notes: 1. It is extremely difficult to emphasise the importance of making certain movements at the same time. The writer has of necessity to describe one thing at a time and it must be realised by the reader that in each attack the foot and arm which is to be raised as a defensive measure move together and at the same speed.

Failure to make this synchronised movement tends to destroy the balance and effectiveness of the movement.

2. The initial step forward or back is a fairly long one. Personally, I am never happy about stepping back. I consider it far more effective and safe to step in to meet a blow aimed at you. However, this is very much a matter of opinion. Both movements are covered in this book.

3. The step forward or back is more than a movement of the leg. The knee of the leg which is advanced is bent and the hips lowered. The resulting position is, or should be, one of perfect balance in which you are firmly braced by the rear leg against being pushed backwards. The knees and hips should be relaxed and springy, providing freedom to move in any direction instantly. A little experiment will show you how it is possible to move freely whilst in a relaxed, well-balanced position. Alternatively, from an awkward or uncomfortable position it is impossible to react without a considerable mental and physical effort.

5. Attacks to Body and Head

IT may well be that in designing the earlier series the
Karate masters intended to do little more than lay down
a series of exercises. I have no doubt that this series is
far stronger and more effective. It follows my own theory
of advancing to meet the attack and continuing to advance
to deal with it by means of a devastating counter. In this
series the shoulder of the striking arm is advanced to add
length and power to the blow.

Attack 1
This is a defence against a blow or kick to your middle
body.

Movement 1
From the Basic Posture raise your left hand towards
your right shoulder and stepping forward with your left
foot sweep your left arm downwards and outwards with
your fist clenched. Alternatively, the edge of the hand can
be used. Your right fist remains at your right hip. The
opponent's right arm or leg is dashed away with the little
finger edge of your fist or forearm. Fig. 31 shows the
position using the clenched fist.

Movement 2
As the attacker's blow is dashed away, step forward
with the right leg and drive your right fist straight forward
to the opponent's chest or face. The left fist is taken back
to the left hip. Fig. 32 shows the counter, but this time the
ward-off is made with the edge of the hand. Return to
the Basic Posture.

Fig. 31   Fig. 32

Movement 3

To defend against a left-handed or left-footed blow to the body step forward with the right foot, raising the right arm to the left shoulder and dashing the blow away with the little finger edge of your forearm, hand or clenched fist. The left fist remains at the left hip (Fig. 31 in reverse).

Movement 4

Step forward with the left leg, driving the left fist to the opponent's chest or face. The right fist is returned to the right hip. Return to the Basic Posture.

Attack 2

Again this is a defence against a blow with foot or arm aimed at the lower part of your body.

Movement 1

The imaginary attacker aims a blow at the lower part of your body with his right hand. Step forward with the left leg, raising the left arm towards your right shoulder and then dashing your arm, with the fist clenched, downwards and outwards, making contact with the little finger edge of the fist or forearm. The right fist is retained at the right hip.

Movement 2
Advance the right foot driving the right fist down into the lower part of the opponent's body, probably his stomach or solar-plexus. The left fist is withdrawn to the left hip. Return to the Basic Posture.

Movement 3
This time defending against a left-handed attack step forward with the right foot, raising the right arm towards the left shoulder and dashing it downwards and outwards to ward-off the blow using the little finger edge of the fist or forearm to make contact. The left fist is held at the left hip.

Movement 4
Step forward with the left foot, driving the left fist into the centre or lower part of the opponent's body and taking the right fist back to the right hip. Finally, resume the Basic Posture.

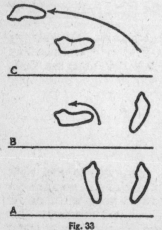

Fig. 33

Attack 3
This attack develops from your left. The blow against which you defend is again delivered to the lower or middle part of the body with a fist or foot.

Movement 1
From the Basic Posture (Fig. 33A) step to your left with your left foot, holding your

right fist at your hip and raising your left hand to your right shoulder to dash it downwards and outwards to ward-off the blow. The contact is made with the little finger edge of the fist or forearm (Fig. 34). Figs. 33A and 33B show the foot movements.

Fig. 34   Fig. 35

Movement 2

Take your right foot past your left (Fig. 33C), driving your right fist to your opponent's face or chest and taking the left fist back to your left hip. Resume the Basic Posture.

Attack 4

An attack from the right.

Movement 1

To meet an attack from the right, step to your right with your right foot, holding your left fist at your left hip whilst raising your right hand to your left shoulder (Fig. 35) to sweep it downwards and outwards. This wards-off a blow or kick aimed at your body at about

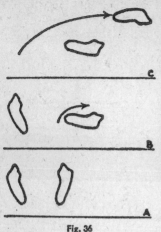

Fig. 36

stomach level. Fig. 35 shows the posture, whilst Fig. 36 shows the foot movement.

Movement 2

Step forward with your left foot (that is you step to your right in respect of your original Basic Posture) (Fig. 36C) taking your right fist to your right hip and driving your left fist to your opponent's face or chest. Return to the Basic Posture.

Attack 5

This attack comes from the rear in the form of a kick or blow to the lower part of the body. In the defence and counter-attack you have to make a complete about turn. Naturally I assume you hear or see the attacker before his blow makes contact with you. The attack is made with the right arm.

Movement 1

From the Basic Posture (Fig. 37A) you pivot on your right foot turning to your left and stepping forward a pace to what was—from your Basic Posture—your rear (Fig. 37B). Your left hand is taken to your right shoulder and swept downwards and outwards to ward-off the attacker's blow. The little finger edge of the fist and forearm make contact. The right fist remains at the right hip.

Movement 2

You now take your right leg past your left, taking the left fist back to the left hip and driving your right fist down into the opponent's stomach (Fig. 37C). Return to the Basic Posture.

Movement 3

This time the attack is made against you with the

opponent's left arm. From the Basic Posture (Fig. 38A) pivot to the right on the left foot stepping to your original rear with your right foot (Fig. 38B). At the same time you

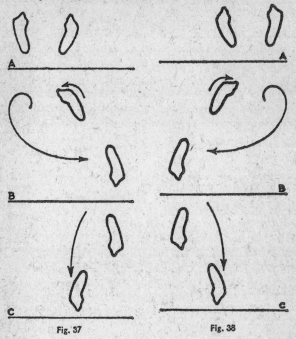

Fig. 37   Fig. 38

raise your right hand to your left shoulder and sweep it downwards and outwards to ward-off the imaginary blow. Your left fist is retained at your left hip.

Movement 4

Complete the turn by stepping to your original rear with your left foot (Fig. 38C) and driving your left fist to the middle of the opponent's body. The right fist is taken down to the right hip. Then resume the Basic Posture.

Attack 6

From the Basic Posture (Fig. 39A) pivot to the left on

the right foot stepping to the left with the left foot and holding the right fist at the hip. The left fist is driven to the middle of the body of the imaginary opponent (Fig. 39B). Resume the Basic Posture.

Attack 7
Attack from the right.

From the Basic Posture (Fig. 40A) pivot to the right on the left foot taking the right foot a pace to the right (Fig. 40B). At the same time hold the left fist at the right hip and drive the right fist to the middle of the opponent's body. Return to the Basic Posture.

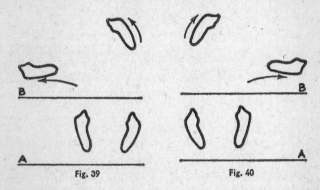

Fig. 39   Fig. 40

Attack 8
Pivot to the left on the left foot advancing the right foot to what was your original left (Fig. 41B). As this is done hold the left fist at the left hip and drive the right fist to the opponent's stomach. Return to the Basic Posture.

Attack 9
An attack from the right.

Pivot to the right on the right foot, stepping to the right with the left foot (Fig. 42B). As you do so retain the right fist at the right hip and drive the left fist to the opponent's stomach. Return to the Basic Posture.

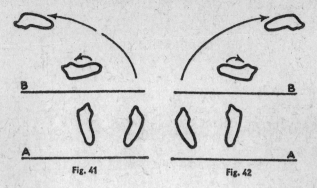

Fig. 41   Fig. 42

Attack 10

Pivot to the left on the left foot stepping to your original left with your right foot. As you do so retain the right fist at the right hip and drive the left fist to the opponent's stomach. (See Fig. 41 for the foot movements.) Return to the Basic Posture.

Attack 11

Attack from the right.

Pivot to the right on the right foot stepping to your original right with the left foot. At the same time retain the left fist at the left hip and drive the right fist to the opponent's stomach. Return to the Basic Posture.

Attack 12

Attack from the left.

Step to your left with your left foot pivoting on your right to do so (Fig. 43B). At the same time hold the right fist at the right hip and bring the left fist up to the vicinity of the right shoulder sweeping it downwards and outwards to ward-off a blow to the middle or lower part of your body. The ward-off is made with the little finger edge of the fist or forearm. Return to the Basic Posture.

K.—3

Attack 13
Attack from the right.

Step to your right with your left foot, pivoting on your right foot to do so. As you pivot retain the left fist at the left hip at the same time taking the right fist to the left shoulder and sweeping it downwards and outwards as if to ward-off a blow to the middle or lower part of the body. The ward-off is made with the little finger edge of the fist or forearm. Return to the Basic Posture.

Attack 14
Attack from the left.

Pivot to your left on the right foot, stepping to the left with the left foot. This time hold the left fist at the left hip and taking the right fist to the left shoulder sweep with it outwards and downwards to ward-off a left-hand blow to the middle or lower body. The little finger edge of the fist and forearm lead and make contact. Resume the Basic Posture.

Attack 15
Attack from the right.

Pivot to the right on the left foot stepping to the right with the right foot, retaining the right fist at the right hip

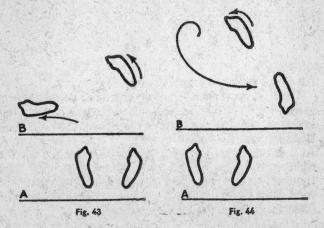

Fig. 43   Fig. 44

and from shoulder level sweeping outwards and downwards with the left fist and forearm, little finger edge
leading. This is to ward-off a right-handed attack to the
lower or middle part of the body. Return to the Basic
Posture.

Attack 16

This movement wards-off an attack from the rear.

Make a complete left about turn to the left on the right
foot stepping to the new front with the left foot as you
do so (Fig. 44). At the same time hold the right fist at the
right hip and sweep the left arm outwards and downwards
to ward-off a right-handed blow to the lower or middle
body. The left fist should be taken to the vicinity of the
right shoulder before the sweep commences. Return to
the Basic Posture.

Attack 17

Another attack from the rear.

Pivot to the right on the left foot stepping round with
your right foot to your new front (Fig. 44 shows this in
reverse). Simultaneously hold the left fist at the left hip
and take your right fist to the level of the left shoulder.
At once sweep it outwards and downwards to ward-off an
attack to the lower or middle body with the opponent's
left fist or foot. Return to the Basic Posture.

Attack 18

An attack from the rear.

The foot movement is exactly the same as that shown
in Fig. 44. To ward-off a left-handed blow or kick to your
lower or middle body turn to the left on the right foot,
stepping back (to your original rear) with your left foot.
At the same time the left fist is held at the left hip and the
right arm is swept downwards and outwards from
shoulder level to ward-off the left-handed attack. The
ward-off is made with the little finger edge of the fist and
forearm. Resume the Basic Posture.

Attack 19

An attack from the rear.

Pivot to the right on the left foot stepping back to your original rear with the right foot (Fig. 44 in reverse). Simultaneously hold the right fist at the right hip and taking the left fist to the level of your right shoulder sweep downwards and outwards with your left arm, little finger edge leading, to ward-off a right-hand blow aimed at your middle or lower body. Return to the Basic Posture.

Note: Do not make too large a circular movement with the arms when warding-off. This takes far too long and leaves the body unprotected. For example, when warding-off a right-hand blow to the stomach in an actual attack, the left fist is moved in a fast, short circle from the left hip towards but not to the left shoulder, and then downwards and outwards. What is required is sufficient movement to develop power, but not enough to take too much time. Do not hold the fists too close to the hips. About twelve inches is a reasonable distance. When teaching, the instructor tells the pupil to take his hand to the shoulder as this is a convenient and easy point to locate.

6. Cuts with the Edge of the Hand

THIS series comprises sweeps with the open hand aimed at the softer parts of the opponent's body. It should be borne in mind that the decision whether to use the open hand or the fist can be made at the very last moment. For example, you might well use an upward sweep to the throat with the open hand, but should it become obvious that you are going to make contact with the side of the jaw it will be better to clench the fist, making contact with the little finger side. In this way you will be far less likely to damage your own hand and the blow is made more effective.

Movement 1

From the Basic Posture step forward with the left foot keeping the right fist at the right hip. The left hand, fingers straight and together, is taken up to the level of the left shoulder and slashed outwards and downwards (Fig. 45). This movement could be used to ward-off a right-handed blow or to attack the left side of the opponent's body. Return to the Basic Posture.

Fig. 45

Movement 2

Step forward with the right foot keeping the left fist at the left hip and taking the right arm, open handed, to the level of the left shoulder. The right arm then sweeps downwards and outwards, little finger edge leading, to ward-off a left-handed blow or to cut at the

53

right side of the opponent's body. Return to the Basic Posture.

Movement 3

Step forward with the left foot, holding the right fist at the right hip and sweeping from the level of the waist upwards and outwards with the left arm, open handed, and with the little finger edge leading. This movement wards-off a right-handed blow to your head or upper body or cuts at the opponent's left armpit or neck. Return to the Basic Posture.

Movement 4

Step forward with the right foot keeping the left fist at the left hip and cutting upwards and outwards with the right arm, open handed, leading with the little finger edge. This sweep wards-off a left-handed blow to your face or chest or delivers a cut to the opponent's neck or right side. Return to the Basic Posture.

Movement 5

Step forward with the left foot, holding the right fist at the right hip. The left hand, fingers open, is taken close to the left hip and then, little finger edge leading, delivers a cut straight forwards and a little upwards to the opponent's groin or stomach. The cut is delivered as if you were attempting to cut an opponent's body into two straight up through the middle. Resume the Basic Posture.

Movement 6

Advance the right foot, retaining the left fist at the left hip and taking the right hand, fingers straight, close to the left hip. The right arm, little finger edge of the hand and forearm leading, sweeps forwards and a little upwards cutting to the imaginary opponent's groin or stomach. Return to the Basic Posture.

The movements which follow are aimed at an opponent who appears at your side.

Movement 7

Step to the left with the left foot, pivoting on the right foot, holding the right fist at the right hip and having taken the left hand near to the right shoulder cut outwards and downwards, little finger edge leading. The blow is used either to ward-off a blow aimed at you or to cut at the opponent's left side or stomach. Return to the Basic Posture.

Movement 8

Step to the right with the right foot, turning on the left, holding the left fist at the left hip and cutting outwards and downwards from shoulder level with the right hand, fingers straight and little finger edge leading. Return to the Basic Posture.

Movement 9

Step to the left with the left foot, turning on the right, keeping the right fist at the hip and cutting upwards and outwards with the little finger edge of the left hand and forearm. Your blow is used either to ward-off an attack or to deliver a cut to the opponent's left side or stomach. Return to the Basic Posture.

Movement 10

Step to your right with your right foot, turning on your left, and retaining your left fist at your hip deliver an upward and outward cut from the vicinity of the left hip with the little finger edge of the right forearm. This cut may ward-off a blow or attack the opponent's stomach or right side. Resume the Basic Posture.

Movement 11

Stepping to your left with your left foot, turning on your right, keep your right fist at the hip and from close to your own right hip sweep forwards and upwards with the little finger cutting edge of your left hand and forearm to the opponent's groin or lower stomach. Return to the Basic Posture.

Movement 12

Step to the right with the right foot, pivoting on the left, keeping the left fist at the hip. The right hand, fingers straight, sweeps from near your left hip upwards and forwards to the opponent's groin or lower part of the stomach. Return to the Basic Posture.

Note: It must be remembered that Karate originated in the East where, particularly in the past, little clothing was worn. In Britain the climate necessitates the wearing of suits and often overcoats with the result that a cut aimed to the body of an attacker at a point listed in a book as vulnerable may well meet a wallet or some other article placed in a pocket which completely blocks the effectiveness of the counter-blow. It is obvious then that Karate used in self-defence, and this after all is the object of the art, must be modified to accord with local conditions. For example, a punch to the body of a clothed opponent is far more likely to be effective than a cut with the edge of the hand.

7. The Use of the Fist and Wrist

THE defence and counter-attacks included in this series call for the use of the weight of the fist and wrist as opposed to the grace of the edge of the hands—bludgeon instead of rapier. It may well be that they are more effective against clothed opponents, and certainly the blow delivered carries more weight. On the other hand there are occasions when the clenched fist is not so effective. This is so, for example, when the blow is to the throat and certainly it is not as easy to grab the attacker's clothing to draw him into a counter-blow when the clenched fist is used as when the attack is warded-off with the open hand.

Many of my comments and notes, such as these, are a matter of personal opinion. These katas or series are intended for training and once the pupil has mastered these he progresses to free-fighting when he develops his own style and techniques, forming opinions of his own.

Movement 1

The opponent aims a blow to your face with his fist.

The first movement is to ward-off a right-hand blow. With your left foot step forward from the Basic Posture, at the same time taking your left arm upwards and outwards, bending your left elbow with the back of the clenched hand facing outwards. The blow is warded away with the left wrist (Fig. 46). Return to the Basic Posture. The wrist is used to ward-off the blow in all the movements in this series.

Movement 2

To ward-off a left-hand blow, step forward from the Basic Posture with the right foot. At the same time take the right arm upwards and outwards, warding off the blow with the right wrist. Resume the Basic Posture.

Note: In movements 1 and 2 the rear foot is not moved at all (see Fig. 46), but in movements 3 and 4 which follow the rear foot must be turned to make the movements possible.

Movement 3

As an attack is made to the head with the right fist from your left side you step to your left from the Basic Posture, turning on your right foot to enable you to do so, at the same time driving your left fist upwards and outwards to ward-off the blow. The foot position is shown in Fig. 47, but the general position is as shown in Fig. 46. Resume the Basic Posture.

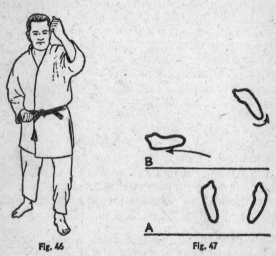

Fig. 46   Fig. 47

Movement 4

This time the attack is a left-hand punch to the head or chest from your right side, with the attacker's left fist. Step to the right, with the right foot, turning the left foot a little to the right to allow you to do so comfortably.

At the same time sweep upwards and outwards with the right arm, warding-off the attack. The blow is warded-off with the wrist. The foot movements are those shown in Fig. 47, but reversed.

Note: The same defence may be made against attacks made from the side whether the attacker punches with his left or right hand. It will be seen that either a left- or right-hand attack can be warded-away with equal effect. The difference comes in the counter-blow. This is covered in the later movements of this series.

Movement 5

A right-hand punch is made to the middle of your body. From the Basic Posture step forward with the left foot, driving outwards and downwards with your left arm, fist clenched. The elbow is bent, with the back of the hand facing outwards. The blow is warded-off with the left wrist (Fig. 48). Resume the Basic Posture.

Fig. 48

Movement 6

This time a left-handed blow is aimed at your middle body. From the Basic Posture step forward with your right foot, driving your right fist outwards and downwards to ward-off the blow. Again the elbow is bent and contact made with your right wrist, the back of which is turned outwards. Return to the Basic Posture.

Movement 7

A right-hand blow is aimed at your middle body from your left. From the Basic Posture step to your left with your left foot, turning on your right as you do so (Fig. 47) driving outwards and downwards with your left arm warding away the blow with the left wrist, which is turned outwards. Resume the basic Posture.

Movement 8

This time a left-handed blow is aimed at your middle body from your right. Step to your right from the Basic Posture with your right foot, turning on your left foot as you do so (Fig. 47 in reverse) warding-off the blow with your right wrist as you drive it outwards and downwards. Finally, return to the Basic Posture.

Note: This rather unusual method of warding-off a blow with the wrist is very effective as the hard wrist is able to disable the opponent's arm as it strikes against the soft part of the forearm. A common question is why not use the fist? This is effective but it means using the extreme end of the defensive weapon and should you misjudge, the blow aimed at you may get through your defence. If, however, you misjudge with the wrist the fist will still ward-off the blow effectively. In addition, the edge of the wrist is harder than the edge of the fist. This "wrist" defence is not advisable against a weapon, as the wrist could then be severely and painfully injured.

The first eight movements demonstrated, and practised, were methods of warding-off blows. The remaining movements follow up with the counter-attacks.

Movement 9

A right-hand punch is aimed at your face or head. From the Basic Posture step forward with the left foot and ward-off the blow with an outwards and upwards sweep of your left fist and arm as in Movement 1. As the left arm sweeps upwards the right fist is driven into the middle of the opponent's body. You can step forward with the right foot, as the counter-punch is made, if necessary. Resume the Basic Posture.

Movement 10

A left-hand punch is aimed at your head or upper body. As in Movement 2 step forward with your right foot from the Basic Posture, warding-off the blow with an upwards and outwards sweep of your right fist and arm. As the blow is warded-off drive your left fist into the opponent's middle body, stepping forward with the left foot if necessary. Resume the Basic Posture.

Movement 11

The attacker aims a right-hand blow to your head or face from your left side. Pivoting on your right foot, step to your left side, warding-off the attack with an upwards and outwards sweep of your left fist and arm. As you ward-off the blow drive your right fist to the middle of the opponent's body, stepping forward with the right foot if required. Resume the Basic Posture.

Movement 12

This defence is against a left-handed blow aimed at your chest or head from your right. Pivot on your left foot, step to your right with your right foot, and sweep your right fist and arm upwards and outwards to ward-off the blow. At the same time drive the left fist into the middle of the attacker's body, stepping forward with the left foot if necessary. Return to the Basic Posture.

Movement 13

This time the attacker aims a right-handed blow to your middle body from your front. Sweep downwards with the left fist and arm, keeping the elbow slightly bent and stepping forward with your left foot as you do so. At the same time counter with a right-handed blow to the stomach, advancing your right foot if necessary.

Note: The counter-punch in movement 13, and also in 14, 15 and 16 which follow, could equally well be a punch to the face or head. This might be better as the arm punching to the head would also provide certain protection from the opponent's other fist. Further alternative counters are described in Movements 19 and 20.

Movement 14

Your attacker aims a left-handed punch at the middle of your body from your front. Sweep your right fist and arm outwards and downwards to ward-off the attack stepping forward with your right foot as you do so. At the same time drive your left fist into the middle of the opponent's body or at his head, stepping forward if required with your left foot. Resume the Basic Posture.

Movement 15

This is a defence against a right-handed blow to your middle body from your left side. Turning on your right foot, step to your left and ward-off the blow with a downwards and outwards sweep of your left fist and arm. Now counter by stepping forward with your right foot and driving your right fist to his middle body or head. Resume the Basic Posture.

Movement 16

This is a defence against a left-handed punch to your middle body from your right side. Pivot to your right on your left foot stepping forward with your right foot and sweeping the attacker's blow away with a downwards and outwards sweep of your right fist and arm. Stepping forward with your left foot punch to the opponent's head or middle body with your left fist. Return to the Basic Posture.

Movement 17

The attacker aims a left-handed punch to your face from your left side. Pivot to your left on your right foot, advancing your left foot and sweeping outwards and upwards with your right fist and arm. Now advancing the right foot, drive your left fist to your opponent's middle body. Resume the Basic Posture.

Movement 18

This defence is against a right-hand blow to the face aimed at you from your right side. Pivot on your left foot to your right, stepping to your right with your right foot and sweeping the blow away with an upwards and outwards sweep of your left fist and arm. Counter by stepping forward with your left foot and driving your right fist into your opponent's middle body. Resume the Basic Posture.

Note: Round arm or "hammer-fist" punches can be used instead of the normal punch as a counter-attack in this series of movements. In this form of counter the side of the fist is swung sideways against the opponent's head or body just as if you were hitting him with a hammer. A blow of this type reaching a vulnerable point is very effective indeed. I will describe two movements using this form of counter, otherwise the movements are identical to Movements 1 and 2 in this series. You will meet this type of counter again in a later series.

Movement 19

The attacker aims a right-hand punch to your head or face from your front. Ward-off the blow by stepping forward with your left foot and sweeping your left fist and arm upwards and outwards. Now take your right fist from your hip to a position close to your left hip and with the fist clenched sweep upwards and a little to your right driving the right side of your fist—the little finger side—against the right side of the opponent's face or jaw. You should step forward with your right foot as you deliver the counter-blow.

Movement 20

This defence is against a left-handed punch to your face or head delivered from your front. From the Basic Posture step forward with your right foot, sweeping upwards and outwards with your right arm and fist to ward-off the blow with, as usual in this series, your right wrist, at the same time taking your left fist across your body from your left to the vicinity of your right hip. Now stepping forward with your left foot, drive your left fist across your body and upwards to strike the left side of his head or jaw with the little finger side of your fist. Return to the Basic Posture.

8. Counters Making Use of the Clothing

ALTHOUGH the first objective of any means of defence must be to ward-off the attack, in Karate you are provided with a series of devastating counter-attacks. Therefore the hand and arm used to ward-off a blow need not be used for that purpose only, although the ward-off must come first. Having warded-off, the hand can catch

Fig. 49

the opponent's arm or clothing and draw him on into a position for a far more effective counter.

It is a serious mistake to attempt to catch the hand, arm or weapon with which the opponent attacks. A defence such as that in Fig. 49, in which the defender is attempting to ward-off a blow with his hand, greatly reduces the effectiveness of the defence and also provides a very good chance of the contact resulting in broken or dislocated fingers or thumb. Compare Fig. 49 with one of the illustrations which show the forearm being used to ward-off a blow. It will be obvious that the latter is far more effective.

However, despite this we still use the warding-off hand to catch the attacker's arm or clothing to draw him into the counter-blow. This either draws him into a more satisfactory position or adds power to the counter, in many cases both. Throughout this series we grip the opponent's arm or jacket with the hand of the warding-off arm in the following way.

The opponent punches at your head with his right fist. You step forward with your left foot, sweeping your left arm, fingers outstretched, upwards and outwards. The blow is warded-off with the little finger edge of the forearm (Fig. 50). At once bend your left wrist and hand round the

Fig. 50

opponent's right arm from above so that you can grip his arm or sleeve (Fig. 51). Now the attacker can be drawn forward in the direction of his punch without any break in his movement. It will be found that in this way not only is he drawn forward without difficulty but he is also drawn towards your left side. This has the double effect of opening his left side to a counter-blow and making it very difficult for him to strike at you with his left arm (Fig. 52). Note that the initial ward-off does not check the attacker's movement but only deflects it. As a result the attacker's forward motion from the blow is continuous as you draw him forward. Any break in the move-

Fig. 51

Fig. 52

ment results in the failure of the defender's own counter-action.

Movement 1

The attacker aims a right-hand punch to your head or upper body. From the Basic Posture step forward with your left foot, sweeping the left arm, fingers extending, upwards and outwards to ward-off the blow (Fig. 50). At once grip his arm or clothing with the left hand and draw him on in the direction of his blow, stepping forward with the right foot and driving your right fist into the side of his body. Resume the Basic Posture. As you draw him forward with your left hand you may find it more effective to turn a little to your left—if so, this should be done.

Movement 2

The attacker aims a left-handed punch at your head or upper body. Step forward with your right foot, sweeping the right arm, with fingers extended, upwards and outwards to ward-off the blow. Without breaking his movement take your right hand over and round the attacker's arm to grip his arm or sleeve and draw him forward in exactly the same direction as his punch, thus guiding him towards your right side. At the same time you step forward with your left foot, if necessary, turning a little to your right and drive your left fist into the right side of his body. Return to the Basic Posture.

Movement 3

This time the attack is a right-handed punch to your stomach or middle body. Step forward with your left foot, sweeping outwards and downwards with your left arm, the fingers being extended, to ward-off the blow with the little finger edge of your forearm. As you make contact turn your arm and hand clockwise in order to grip the inside of his sleeve or arm and draw him forward in the direction of his punch. Now, possibly turning a little to your left, step forward with your right leg and drive your

right fist into the stomach area or left side of the opponent.
Resume the Basic Posture.

Movement 4

This counter is against a left-hand punch to your middle
body. As the attacker punches, ward-off his blow by
stepping forward with your right foot and sweeping
outwards and downwards with your right arm, the
fingers being extended. By turning your wrist and forearm
anti-clockwise grip the inside of his sleeve or arm and
draw him forward in the direction of his blow, turning a
little to your right as you do so, if necessary. As you draw
him on advance your left leg and drive your left fist into
the middle or right side of his body. Return to the Basic
Posture.

Movement 5

The defence this time is against a downward blow such
as may be made by an opponent attacking your head with

Fig. 53

a stick. For practice purposes the attacker uses his
clenched fist. The attack is made with the right hand and
is warded-off by stepping forward with the left foot and

sweeping the left arm, fingers extended, upwards and a little sideways. To ward-off downward blows the sweeping arm is kept a little more bent than against a straight blow (Fig. 53). The arm or sleeve is caught by turning the arm and hand clockwise and drawn downwards and to the defender's left, thus turning the attacker a little to his left. This exposes the front of his body and the attack is countered by stepping forward with the right foot and driving the right fist into his middle body. If he has not turned sufficiently the counter-punch is made to his left side. Now return to the Basic Posture.

Movement 6

The attack is a downward blow to the head made with the left arm. Ward-off with an upwards and outwards sweep of the right arm, stepping forward with the right foot as you do so. Turning the right arm a little anticlockwise, grip the inside of his arm or sleeve and draw it downwards and to your right, thus turning him a little to his right. Advancing your left foot drive your left

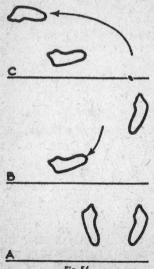

Fig. 54

fist into the middle of his body or his right side. Resume the Basic Posture.

Movement 7

Defence against a right-hand blow to the head or upper body from your left side. Step to your left with your left foot (Fig. 54B), sweeping upwards and outwards with your left hand, fingers extended. Turning the hand and forearm clockwise grip the top of his sleeve or arm and draw it forward in the direction of his blow. Counter by advancing the right foot (Fig. 54C) and driving your right fist into the opponent's middle body or left side. Now return to the Basic Posture.

Movement 8

The attacker aims a left-handed blow to your head or upper body from your left side. Step to your left with your left foot (Fig. 54B), sweeping upwards and outwards with your left arm, keeping the fingers extended. By turning the wrist and hand clockwise grip the outside of his arm or sleeve and draw him forward in the direction of his blow. This will tend to turn his back to you. Now step forward with the right foot (Fig. 54C) and drive your right fist into his back or left side. Resume the Basic Posture.

Movement 9

Here we have the counter to a right-hand blow to the head or upper body from the right side. At once step to the right with your right foot, sweeping upwards and outwards with your left arm to ward-off the attack. As you do so turn your wrist or hand clockwise to grip the inside of his arm. Simultaneously step forward (to your original right) with your left foot, driving your right fist into the attacker's middle body. Resume the Basic Posture.

Movement 10

This time the counter is against a left-handed blow to the head from the right. Step to the right with the right foot, sweeping upwards and outwards with the right arm. As you do so turn the wrist and hand slightly clockwise to grip the top or inside of his arm or sleeve and draw him forward in the direction of his blow. At the same time step forward to your original right with your left foot, driving your left fist into his back or right side. Resume the Basic Posture.

Note: Where I have described a clockwise or anti-clockwise turn of the wrist the reader might find the opposite equally effective or more natural. The result of reversing the turn is that another part of the opponent's sleeve is gripped. I have described what I consider more effective.

9. The Use of the Feet and Knees in Karate.

READERS may well consider the use of the feet and knees as "un-British" but in my opinion anyone who attacks any innocent member of the public deserves anything he receives. The feet are excellent weapons because the legs are longer than the arms and thus give you a defensive weapon longer than the attacker's reach or at least just as long should he be using a weapon such as a stick against you. In addition, as you will be likely to be wearing shoes, you also have a weapon far harder than your fist or edge of the hand. The knees are weapons which are invaluable in close fighting which might well develop should your arms be held or ineffective because of loss of balance or a bad position. As a blow with the knee is usually directed upwards at the lower parts of the body it is very difficult to check with the hands and arms.

The use of the legs and feet in Karate requires considerable training and practice. It is not just a matter of kicking the opponent's shins. A really good Karateman can kick well above the level of the top of his own head, without losing his balance backwards, and almost as high sideways.

Attack 1
The following movements are made with the leg from the Basic Posture to which you return after each movement.

Movement 1
Step forward with the left leg, immediately kicking forwards and upwards with the right (Fig. 55).

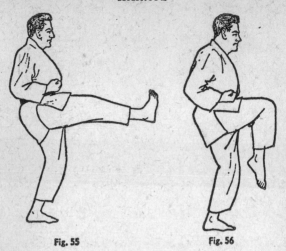

Fig. 55   Fig. 56

Movement 2

Step forward with the right leg, immediately kicking forwards and upwards with your left foot.

Movement 3

Step to your left with your left foot turning in that direction and kick forwards and upwards with your right so as to attract an opponent who would be attacking you from your left side.

Movement 4

Step to the right with your right foot, kicking upwards and forwards with your left foot to attack an opponent at your right side.

Note: In each of these four movements the kick should be aimed at the opponent's head or face.

The next four counter-attacks are made with the knee and are aimed at the middle of the opponent's body.

Movement 5

Step forward with the left foot, immediately bringing up the right knee to the middle of the body of an imaginary opponent (Fig. 56).

Movement 6

Step forward with the right foot and drive the left knee forward and up into the middle of the opponent's body.

Movement 7

The right knee drives upwards and outwards to your right to make contact with the middle of the opponent's body or the outside of his right thigh. Naturally the front or any side of the opponent's thigh is an equally effective target should he have turned to offer such a target (Fig. 57).

Fig. 57   Fig. 58

Movement 8

The left knee is driven upwards and to your left to make contact with the opponent's middle body or thigh. The outside of his thigh is the usual target.

Now the heel is used as the counter-weapon, the counter-attack being delivered to the front or side of the opponent's knee.

K.—4

Movement 9

This is a simple movement, the toes being held back and the kick delivered with the right heel to the front of the attacker's knee. Either to the left or right knee as convenient (Fig. 58).

Movement 10

This is the movement shown in Fig. 58 in reverse. The toes of the left foot are drawn back and the kick delivered with the left heel to the front of the attacker's left or right knee as convenient.

Next we have the side of the foot used as the counter-weapon. Although all Karate instruction manuals include this type of counter, usually illustrated in bare feet, I personally consider that the side of the unshod foot is too susceptible to injury to be used as an effective weapon. When shoes are worn, however, the position is very different. The hard edge of a shoe making contact with the muscles of the leg can cause considerable pain.

Movement 11

The attacker is at your right side. Bring the right foot up so that the knee is raised and your foot is in front of your left knee-cap (Fig. 59). Then with the right edge of the foot deliver a powerful sideways kick to the outside of the opponent's thigh or to his side (Fig. 60).

Movement 12

The attacker is at your left side. Bring your left foot up to the front of your right knee, raising your left knee as you do so and kick sideways and upwards with the outside edge of your left foot, aiming at the outside of the opponent's knee or the side of his body.

Movement 13

The attacker kicks upward at your body with his right foot. If the movement can be anticipated it can be very effectively blocked and countered in the same movement

Fig. 59   Fig. 60

by turning the toes of the right foot inwards and drawing up the right knee in front of the left thigh. Now the inside edge of the right foot is brought down into the attacker's shin as he kicks upwards.

Movement 14

This is a blocking and counter-kick with the left foot. The left foot is turned inwards, the knee being brought up in front of the right thigh. As the attacker kicks, the inside of the left foot is thrust against his shin.

In the movements which follow you have the advantage that you make use of the longest possible natural weapon, but on the other hand you are compelled to turn your back on the attacker when using this form of defence.

Movement 15

As the opponent comes forward to attack, perhaps using a downward blow at your head with a weapon, pivot on the left foot, to the left, bending the left knee as you do so and thrust backwards with your right heel at the attacker's knee, thigh or middle body (Fig. 61).

Movement 16

This time the left heel is used to counter. As the
attack is made pivot to the right on the right foot, driving
the left heel back to the opponent's middle body, knee or
thigh.

Fig. 61

Movement 17

This form of counter-attack, so popular in professional
wrestling, is illustrated in practically all Karate books
but requires a trained athlete to carry it out. This is
called the "Jump Kick" in Karate and the "Drop Kick"
in professional wrestling. In this method you turn your
right side towards the opponent and kick with the right
foot to the opponent's head. As you do so the left foot is
thrown up as well and both feet are driven to his head.

In the next movements the opponent has gripped your
clothing or wrist with his hand preparatory to pulling
you into position for a blow with his other hand, etc.

Movement 18

The opponent grips your clothing fairly low down with
his right hand. Balancing on your left foot bring up your

right knee as high as possible, bending the leg, and drive the knee down on to the opponent's wrist.

Movement 19

The opponent grips fairly low on your clothing with his left hand. Balancing on the right foot and bending the left knee raise it as high as possible and bring it down on the opponent's left wrist.

Movement 20

The attacker grips your left wrist or sleeve. Swing your left arm in a circle outwards to your left and downwards. As the attacker's arm is brought downwards bring the right knee up and then down on his wrist.

Movement 21

Your right wrist or sleeve is held. Take your right arm outwards to your right and downwards in a circular movement. As the attacker's arm is brought downwards raise your left knee and drive it downwards onto the attacker's wrist.

Note: It is extremely important when using the knee or foot to counter-attack that you bring your foot down to the ground as soon as possible after making the counter-movement. This is because of the danger of the leg you are using to kick being grabbed and pulled away, throwing you off balance. Also the foot on which you are standing can be swept away. Throughout these Karate movements I have emphasised that you should return to your well-balanced Basic Posture after each movement. This is particularly important after using the leg in a counter-attack.

10. Counters With the Foot and Knee

IN this chapter I will be dealing with the use of the foot and knee as counter-weapons after the opponent's attack has been warded-off with the arm or the arm has been used not only to ward-off, but also to pull the attacker into the counter-blow.

Attack 1
The opponent, with his right arm, aims a blow to your head or upper body.

Movement 1
The blow is warded-off with an upwards and outwards sweep of the left arm, fingers extended. At the same time you step forward with your left foot. As the blow is warded-off bring the right knee up into the attacker's middle body or left side should he have turned.

Movement 2
The blow is again warded-off as you step forward with the left foot with an upwards and outwards sweep of the left arm, fingers extended. As you ward-off the blow turn the wrist clockwise and grip the inside of the attacker's right sleeve, pulling him in the direction of his blow. This will turn him so that his front is towards you. Counter with an upward drive of your right knee to the middle of his body.

Movement 3
As for Movement 2 ward-off the blow with an outwards and upwards sweep of the left hand, drawing the attacker in the direction of his blow by a pull on his sleeve. Now bring the left knee up into his middle body or right side.

Movement 4

The attacker again uses his right arm to your head or upper body but this time you ward-off the blow with an upwards and outwards sweep of your right arm. To do this the right fist is taken from the Basic Posture to the left hip before the sweep commences. As the blow is deflected the attacker tends to turn his back on you so that the left knee can be driven into the base of his spine or his back.

Attack 2

This is the counter to a left-handed blow to the head or upper body.

Movement 1

Ward-off the blow with an upwards and outwards sweep of the right hand and arm, keeping the fingers straight and stepping forward with the right foot as you do so. Immediately bring up the left knee into the opponent's middle body, or right side should he have turned, as his blow was deflected.

Movement 2

Deflect the left-handed blow with an upwards and outwards sweep of the right arm, stepping in with the right foot. The fingers are extended. As you ward-off the blow turn the hand and wrist anti-clockwise to grip the inside of the sleeve or arm and draw him forward in the direction of his blow. Counter by driving your left knee upwards into the front of his body.

Movement 3

Ward-off the blow as in Movement 2 but this time counter by driving the right knee up into the attacker's middle body or left side.

Movement 4

Ward-off the left-handed blow to the head by taking the left fist from the Basic Posture at the right hip across to the left hip and then sweeping upwards and across your

body. This deflects the blow past your left shoulder.
Step forward with the left foot as the warding-off action
is made. Counter with an upward drive of the right knee
to the base of the spine or back.

Attack 3

These movements are defences to kicks.

Movement 1

The opponent kicks to your middle body with his right
foot. As he does so ward-off the kick with a downwards
and outwards sweep of your right arm, fingers extended,

Fig. 62

stepping in with your right foot as you do so. This leaves
the opponent standing on his left foot with his right leg
stretched forward at hip-level or higher (Fig. 62). Counter
by driving the left knee into the base of the opponent's
spine.

Movement 2

This is exactly the same defensive action to a right-foot
kick to your middle body described in Movement 1, but
do not step in with the right foot. This time the counter
is a left-foot kick to the side of the opponent's body. This

can only be done if there is sufficient space between you and the attacker. It is to provide this space that you do not step in.

Movement 3

Again the right-footed kick to your middle body. This time step in with the left foot and ward-away the attack with an outward and downward sweep with the left arm. This takes the opponent's right leg outwards and upwards. Immediately counter with an upward drive of the right knee to the groin, which is fully exposed by your deflection of the kick.

Attack 4

The opponent attacks with a left-foot kick to your middle body from the front.

Movement 1

As the left-foot kick is delivered ward-away his leg with a downwards and outwards sweep of your left arm, stepping in with your left leg. Counter with an upward drive of your right knee to the base of his spine.

Movement 2

Ward-off the left-foot kick to your middle body with a downwards and outwards sweep of the left arm but do not step in with the left foot. As there is now a reasonable distance between you and your opponent, counter by kicking to his left side with your right foot.

Movement 3

Deflect the left-footed kick to your body by sweeping outward and downward with your right arm, stepping in with your right foot as you do so. As this ward-off pushes his left leg outward, drive your left knee upwards into his groin.

Attack 5

These are counters to the face against an opponent who has attacked from your front and who, after his attack has been deflected, is close to you.

Movement 1

The attacker punches to your head or upper body with his right fist. Step in with the left foot, deflecting the blow with an outwards and upwards sweep of your left arm. As you do so bring your right arm round his head from the outside, pull down his head and counter by driving your right knee upwards into his face.

Movement 2

The attack is a left-handed punch to your head or upper body. Step in with the right foot, warding-off the blow with an outwards and upwards sweep of your right arm. As you do so take your left arm round the opponent's neck from the outside pulling his head down so that you can counter with an upward drive of your left knee to his face (Fig. 63).

Fig. 63

Movement 3

You are attacked with a right-footed kick to the middle body from your front. Step in with your left foot sweeping away the kick with an outwards and downwards sweep of your left arm. As you do so take your right arm round his neck from the outside and pull his head down sufficiently to enable you to counter by driving your right knee up into his face.

Movement 4

To counter a left-footed kick to your middle body from the front, step forward with your right foot, warding-off the blow with a downwards and outwards sweep of the right arm. As the leg is warded-away take your left arm round your opponent's neck from the outside and pull his head downwards. Counter-attack by driving your left knee upwards into his face.

Movement 5

This attack is a downward blow to the top of your head, probably with a stick. The attack is made with the right arm. Deflect the blow past your left shoulder with an upwards and outwards sweep of your left arm, stepping in as you do so with your left foot. Do not stop the downward travel of the arm but with an anti-clockwise twist of your wrist, grip the sleeve and pull the arm downward in the direction of the blow. The attacker is now bent forward. Increase this by putting your right hand on his head and pulling forward and down. Counter by driving the right knee upwards into his face.

Movement 6

You are attacked with a downward blow to the head with the left hand. The opponent would no doubt be armed with a stick to make such an attack. Deflect the blow past your right shoulder with an outwards and upwards sweep of your right arm, stepping in with your right foot as you do so. By turning your right wrist clockwise catch his arm and draw it down in the direction of his blow, thus curving the opponent's body forward. Increase this curve by placing your left hand on the top of his head or behind it and pull his head forward and downwards. Counter-attack by driving your left knee upwards into the attacker's face.

Note: It is essential to obtain maximum power from the drive of the knee. Although the strength of the thigh always ensures considerable power, the force and speed of the blow can be increased if the toes of the foot are pointed downwards (Fig. 63).

11. The Use of the Elbows

THE elbows are valuable weapons particularly when you are beside your opponent. They can be more useful than the knee which, although it delivers a far heavier blow, tends to be rather restricted for other than frontal attacks. As most blows are delivered to the front or back it is seldom realised how vulnerable the sides of the head, body and thigh are to attack. A few minutes' experiment on yourself will soon show you how many vulnerable spots there are on the side of the body.

Fig. 64

Attack 1
Your opponent attacks with his right arm to your head or upper body.

Movement 1
Step forward to the opponent's right side with the left foot, warding-off the blow with an upwards and outwards sweep of the left arm, fingers extended. As soon as your left foot returns to the ground step forward with the right foot, taking it to your left of the opponent's right foot and drive your right elbow outwards to the side of his body (Fig. 64). To attack with the right elbow the right hand is taken back to the top of the left shoulder in order to develop maximum power for the blow. To this

counter can be added a blow with the right knee. Instead of advancing your right foot outside that of your opponent, step between your opponent's feet with the right foot driving the knee up into his groin following up with the elbow to the body.

Movement 2

As in Movement 1 advance the left foot to the opponent's left side, warding-off the blow with an upwards and outwards sweep with your left arm. As the left foot is placed on the ground advance the right past the outside of the opponent's right foot and taking the right fist up above the right shoulder, drive the elbow outwards and downwards into the side of the attacker's neck. Again there is the alternative of bringing the right foot between the opponent's feet and driving the knee upwards into his groin, as the elbow drives into his neck.

Attack 2

The attacker aims a left-handed blow to your head or upper body.

Movement 1

Step forward to his left side with your right foot, warding-off the blow with an upwards and outwards sweep of your right arm. As your right foot is replaced on the mat take the left foot past the outside of his left foot and taking the left fist above the right shoulder, drive your elbow outwards to the side of his body. Alternatively, you can step forward between his feet with your left foot and counter with an upward drive of the left knee to his groin.

Movement 2

As for Movement 1 step to his left side with your right foot, warding-off his blow with an upwards and outwards sweep of your right arm. Immediately you replace your right foot on the ground, step outside the attacker's left foot with your left foot and taking your left fist above your right shoulder drive the elbow outwards to the side of his neck. Alternatively, instead of moving your left

foot outside his left foot, step with it between his feet
and deliver a blow to his groin with your left knee as a
second counter-attack.

Attack 3
You are attacked with a right-handed blow to the head
or upper body from your right side.

Movement 1
As the punch is delivered step to your right with your
right foot, warding-off the blow with an upward and outward sweep of your right arm. The foot movement from
the Basic Posture (Fig. 65A) is shown in Fig. 65B. As the

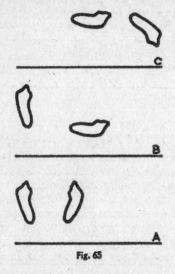

Fig. 65

right foot is replaced on the mat step to your original
right with your left foot, taking it in front of and across
your right (Fig. 65C). Taking the right fist close to the
right shoulder deliver an outward blow to the side or
back of the opponent's body with the left elbow.

Movement 2
The same as for Movement 1 but after moving your

left foot in front of and across your right as shown in Fig. 65C, drive your right knee upwards into the outside of your opponent's right thigh. Should he not have turned sufficiently to his left to enable you to do this, drive the knee into his groin.

Attack 4

The attacker delivers a left-handed blow to your head or upper body from your left side.

Movement 1

To ward-off the punch, step to your left with your left foot, sweeping your left arm upwards and outwards to deflect the blow. As you replace your left foot on the mat take your right foot in front of, and across, your left. Simultaneously take your left fist close to your left shoulder and by driving the right elbow outwards deliver a blow to the side or back of the opponent's body. The foot movements are like those shown in Fig. 65 but reversed.

Movement 2

This is very similar to Movement 1 in that the blow is warded-off with an upwards and outwards sweep of the left arm as you step to your left with your left foot. Again you might take the left fist close to the left shoulder and drive the elbow outwards into the middle of the opponent's body as a secondary counter-attack, but this time, after stepping forward with the right foot, the left knee is driven upwards into the outside of his left thigh, or, should he not have turned sufficiently, into his groin.

Attack 5

The attacker grips you from behind round your arms and body. Bend your knees to lower your body and drive your elbow outwards and upwards. This loosens, or may even break, the grip round your arms (Fig. 66). Turn a little to your right and drive your right elbow backwards into the middle of the attacker's body. You could equally well turn to your left and drive the left elbow backwards into his body.

Attack 6

The attacker grips you round the body from behind but leaves your arms free. In this position you cannot reach him with your arms or elbows so have to loosen his grip. To do this raise both your arms forward, with the knuckles facing downwards (Fig. 67), and drive your

Fig. 66   Fig. 67

fists down onto the backs of his forearms, hands or wrists. The blow is delivered with the knuckles of the fore and middle fingers. As he loosens his grip turn a little to the right and drive your right elbow upwards into the side of his head or downwards into the middle or side of his body. Alternatively, turn to the left and make a similar attack to his left side with your left elbow. To attack with the elbow the fist is taken up above the opposite shoulder before it is driven into the opponent.

Attack 7
Movement 1
You are held from behind by an opponent who throws his

arm round your neck and pulls you backwards. Do not worry too much about being pulled back but turn to your right, pushing your hips back as you make the turn. You will find that as your turn is completed you will have recovered balance. The turn continues until you have your right side towards your opponent when you drive your right elbow into his right side. To deliver the blow, the right fist should be taken across the body and above the left shoulder in order to develop power for the counter-attack.

Movement 2

This is identical to Movement 1 except that you turn to your left and deliver the blow with the elbow with your left arm to his left side. It does not matter which way you turn when you are held round the neck from behind. It may be better to turn right when it is the opponent's left arm which is round your neck and to your left when he uses his right, but this makes very little difference. In addition you may not be able to tell which arm is being used. The main object must be to move rapidly. There is no point in passing out whilst you consider which way to turn.

Note: When delivering the blows with the elbow it is essential to take the arm first across the body. This provides space for the blow to gather momentum. Far greater power is added to an elbow blow if the hand of the arm delivering the blow is clenched. As you take your fist from the Basic Posture, where it is lightly clenched, you clench it firmly to harden the muscles for your attack.

12. Dealing with Repeated or Successive Attacks

So far in this book the movements I have described have consisted of only one blow which has been warded-off and then countered with a single blow. This of course is not realistic. You may well have to deal with several successive blows before the opportunity is provided for your counter. Similarly you may have to deliver more than one blow against your opponent before he is rendered unable to continue his attack. This will be made obvious when you join a good club and take part in free practice. In this free practice you simulate a fight in which all Karate movements are used, but the blows are "pulled" just short of their target. Each contestant is expected to call out "Maitta," that is "I am beaten" in acknowledgement of a blow which would have landed. In this chapter I will deal with two successive attacks which have to be warded-off before a counter-blow can be attempted. In a subsequent chapter I will describe successive counter-blows.

Attack 1
The opponent attacks with a right-handed blow to the head or upper body followed by a left-handed blow to the same target.

Movement 1
As the opponent punches with his right hand, step in with the left foot and ward-off the blow with an upwards and outwards sweep of the left arm, fingers extended (Fig. 68). The left-hand blow is avoided by a similar upwards and outwards sweep of the right arm, stepping in with the right

foot if there is space. To counter, turn the right arm anti-clockwise and drive the little finger side of the left hand down to the right side of his neck. An alternative to this

Fig. 68

is to clench the left fist and by turning it anti-clockwise deliver a hammer-fist blow with the little finger side of the fist to the top of the opponent's head or his right temple.

Movement 2

The two punches are warded-off exactly as described in Movement 1 but this time do not step in with the right foot and instead of using the right arm to counter-attack, you drive your right knee into the attacker's groin.

Attack 2

The attack is made with successive left and right punches to the head.

Movement 1

The left arm is warded-off with an outwards and upwards sweep of the right arm, fingers extended, stepping in with the right foot. The right-hand punch which follows is deflected with a similar sweep of the left arm—step in with the left foot if space permits. The attacker now has both of his arms pushed outwards and upwards and you counter by turning the left wrist anti-clockwise and attacking to his neck with the little finger side of the fist.

Movement 2

The attack is warded-off in exactly the same manner with outward and upward sweeps of the right and left arms. This time, as the second blow is warded-off, do not step in but instead drive the left knee into the attacker's groin.

Attack 3

The attacker punches to the head or upper body with his right arm and follows up with a left-handed punch to the stomach.

Movement 1

The punch to the head with the right hand is warded-off with an upwards and outwards sweep of the left arm, the fingers being extended. You should step in as you ward-off this blow. The left-hand punch to the stomach is warded-off with a downwards and outwards sweep of the right arm, the fingers of which are also extended. Step in with the right foot if there is room. Your left arm is now turned anti-clockwise and the little finger edge of the hand is swept down across the right side of his neck. As an alternative, the left fist can be clenched and the little finger side of the fist crashed down on the attacker's head or temple in hammer-fist fashion.

Movement 2

The right-arm punch to the head and left-arm punch to the stomach are warded-off as in Movement 1 with successive sweeps of the left and right arms. As before, you step in with the left foot as you sweep away his blow to the head with your left arm, but this time as you ward-off the left-hand punch to the stomach you hold the leg back, driving your right knee into the attacker's groin.

Attack 4

You are attacked with successive blows. The first a left-hand punch to the head and the second a right-hand punch to the stomach.

Movement 1

The left-handed punch to the head is warded-off with an upwards and outwards sweep with the right arm, fingers extended. Step forward with the right foot as you make the sweep. As the second attack is made to the stomach with the right arm, deflect the attack with a downwards and outwards sweep with the left hand. The fingers should be extended. Step in with the left foot as you sweep if there is space. Now turn your right wrist clockwise and sweep the little finger edge of the right hand down to the left side of the attacker's neck. There are two alternatives. You can clench your right fist and crash the fist down to the opponent's head or temple. Contact should be made with the little finger edge of the fist. The second alternative is to clench the right fist and bending the arm at the elbow drive the right elbow and upper forearm to the attacker's face.

Movement 2

The successive punches are warded-off in exactly the way I have described in Movement 1 but as you make the deflecting sweep with the left arm you do not step in. Instead you point the toes of your left foot downwards and drive your left knee upwards into the attacker's groin.

Attack 5

In this attack you meet the drive of the opponent's knee to your groin. At close quarters this is a very difficult attack to deflect especially should it be a second attack made when your attention is concentrated on the first. This is the case in this defence in which your opponent drives his right fist to your head and follows up with his knee to your body. Which knee does not matter particularly as the defence is the same.

Movement 1

Ward-off the right-hand punch to the head by stepping forward with your left foot and sweeping upwards and outwards with your left arm, keeping the fingers extended. Now as the attacker drives one of his knees up to your body bring your own left knee upwards and to your right (Fig. 69) so that the point of your knee meets the side of the attacker's knee or leg. This not only wards-off the blow but also disables his leg. Now step in with your right foot and drive your right knee to the opponent's groin.

Fig. 69

Note: As you have warded-off the attack with your left arm it is essential to deflect the knee attack with your left knee as the left knee can attack the side of the opponent's knee, either the inside or outside of his knee, depending on which knee he uses for his attack. If, alternatively, you used your right knee you would be likely to find your knee meeting his, which might well disable you or at the best cause you considerable pain. This is because stepping forward with the left foot as you ward-off turns your body a little to your right.

Movement 2

This is exactly the same as for Movement 1 in that you ward-off the blow and drive off the knee attack with your own left knee. At this stage, instead of countering with your right knee, you clench your right fist and, stepping in with your right foot, drive your right fist to the middle of his body.

Alternatives:

(a) Clench your right fist and bending your arm at the elbow dash your elbow into the opponent's face.

(b) Extend the fingers of your right hand and taking the

right arm above your left shoulder use a side hand cut to the right side of the opponent's neck.

(c) Extend the fingers of the right hand and thrust the fingertips to the opponent's throat or face.

(d) Turn the left wrist, after warding-off the attack of the right fist, anti-clockwise and make a side hand cut to the right side of the opponent's neck.

(e) Clench the left hand after deflecting the right hand, and, turning your wrist anti-clockwise, make a hammer-fist attack to the right side of the opponent's head or temple.

Attack 6

Your opponent attacks with a left-handed punch to your face or upper body and follows up by attempting to drive his knee (either knee) to your groin.

Movement 1

As the opponent delivers his left-handed punch step in with your right foot, sweeping it upwards and outwards with your right arm to deflect the blow. Your fingers should be extended. Now as he attacks to your body with his knee drive your own right knee upwards and inwards, making contact with the side of his knee or leg. Now drive your left knee into the groin of your opponent.

Movement 2

As for Movement 1 you ward-off the left-handed attack to the head with an upwards and outwards sweep of your right hand, extending the fingers, and stepping in with your right foot as you do so. Ward-off the knee attack by driving your own right knee upwards and inwards and immediately step in with your left foot, driving your left fist into his middle body.

Alternatives:

These are exactly the same as for Movement 1 except that left must be read for right and right for left throughout.

Attack 7

The assailant drives his right arm down to your head, no

doubt attempting to hit the top of your head with a
weapon such as a stick. He follows up by driving his head
into your face.

Movement 1

The downward attack of the right arm is warded-off by
stepping forward with the left foot and sweeping upwards and outwards with the left arm, keeping the fingers
extended. Now as the attacker lowers his head to butt you
in the face, move forward with your right foot, and clenching your right fist and bending that arm at the elbow, drive
the elbow upwards and forwards into his face. This is
similar to the counter-attack shown in Fig. 75. This
defence, which itself is an effective counter-attack,
straightens the attacker and places him in an ideal position for you to counter by driving your right knee upwards and forwards into his groin.

Movement 2

The defence is as for Movement 1. The downward blow is
warded-off with an upward and outward sweep of your
left arm as you step in with the left foot, and the butt to
the face crashed away with the right forearm and elbow.
This attempt to butt results in the attacker bending
forward, providing you with the opportunity to deliver a
downward cut with the little finger edge of the left hand
to the back of his neck or a hammer-fist blow with the
same hand down to the back of his head or neck.

Movement 3

The defence is exactly the same as for Movements 1 and
2. The ward-off with the left hand and the drive to the
face with the right elbow or forearm are to repel the butt
to your own face. This time, however, instead of stepping
forward with your right foot as you counter with your
right elbow and forearm, you point the toes of your right
foot downwards and drive the knee up into the attacker's
groin at the same time as, or immediately after, driving
your elbow to the face. It is worth noting that the counter-
attack has to be made with your right foot as when your

assailant made his initial downward attack with his right arm, he will have advanced his right foot, blocking any attack of your left knee to his groin. Even should he have opened himself up again by advancing his left foot as he attempted the butt the elbow drive of your right arm and drive of the left knee tend to be two separate movements, whilst a concerted drive of your right hand and elbow can be made simultaneously as one.

Attack 8

You are attacked with a downward blow to your head with the opponent's left arm followed by an attempt to drive his head into your face.

Movement 1

At once step in with the right foot, sweeping upwards and outwards with the right arm to deflect away the attack. As he attempts to drive his head to your face, move in with your left foot, clench your left fist, bend the arm and drive your left elbow and forearm upwards into his face.

Movement 2

Defend in exactly the way I have described in Movement 1. Block the left-hand blow with an upwards and outwards sweep of the right hand and his attempt to butt you in the face with an upward drive of your left elbow and forearm into his face. As the attempt to butt has resulted in his leaning forward you are able to add an additional counter by bringing down the little finger edge of your right hand to the back of his neck or driving your right fist down in a hammer-fist attack to the back of his head or neck.

Movement 3

Again the defence is as for Movement 1. The ward-off with the right arm by means of an upwards and outwards sweep followed by the drive of the left elbow and forearm to his face as he attempts the butt. At the same time that you drive your elbow to his face, bring your left knee forward and upward to his groin, pointing your toes downwards as you do so.

Attack 9

Your assailant attempts to drive his right fist into your stomach and follows up with a left-handed blow to your head or upper body.

Movement 1

As your opponent drives his right fist to your stomach ward it off with a downwards and outwards sweep of your left arm. This is made by taking your left fist from your left hip (Basic Posture) to your right shoulder and commencing the sweep. As you sweep, step forward with your left foot. At once ward-off the left-hand punch to your head with an upwards and outwards sweep of your right arm. The result of these two defensive sweeps is to drive both his arms outwards, leaving your own arms in a good position inside his for a counter which he cannot ward-off. At once counter-attack by driving your left arm, which having swept downwards, has been returned to its basic position, upwards to drive your elbow and forearm into his face; move in with your left foot as you do so if this is possible. As you stepped in with that foot in your original counter any further advance with it may not be possible However, even a slight forward movement adds power to the blow.

Movement 2

The two successive blows are warded-off as for Movement 1, your left arm sweeping downwards and outwards and your right sweeping upwards and outwards. This time counter-attack by using your upraised right hand to deliver an edge-of-the-hand blow with the little finger edge to the left of his neck. As an alternative you can clench your right fist and deliver a hammer-fist blow to the side or top of his head.

Movement 3

Again ward-off the successive right- and left-arm attacks with the defensive sweeps of your left arm downwards and outwards and your right outwards and upwards as fully described in Movement 1. This time take advantage of the weak position by driving either knee upwards and

forwards into his groin. The knee to be used will depend
on the position of yourself and your opponent.

Attack 10

You are attacked with a left-handed blow to the stomach
immediately followed by a right-handed punch to the
head or upper body.

Movement 1

Ward-off the left-hand punch to the stomach by taking
your right hand close to your left shoulder and then sweeping your arm outwards and downwards. The second
attack to your head with his right arm is warded-off with
an upwards and outwards sweep of your left arm. At once
bend your right arm, which has been returned to the
basic position, at the elbow and counter with an upward
drive of your elbow and forearm to the opponent's face.

Movement 2

Ward-off the blows as described in Movement 1. As a
result your right fist is placed low at your right side whilst
your left is held above your left shoulder. Immediately
turn your left forearm anti-clockwise and deliver a side-
hand cut down to the side of the opponent's neck. Instead
of the cut you can clench your left fist and deliver a
hammer-fist blow to the side of his neck or the top of his
head.

Movement 3

Again his left-hand attack to the stomach is swept away
with a downwards and outwards sweep of your right arm.
His right-hand blow to the head is warded-off outwards
and upwards by your left arm. At once counter by driving
the knee, whichever is better positioned, upwards and
forwards into the groin, pointing the toes of the foot
downwards as you do so.

Attack 11

The attacker attempts a right-footed kick to your groin
and follows up with a right-handed punch to your head
or upper body.

Movement 1

As the attacker delivers his upward right-footed kick to your groin sweep it away with a downwards and outwards sweep with the little finger edge of your left hand, keeping the fingers extended. A hammer-fist blow would be equally effective—perhaps more so. This attack having failed he replaces his foot on the ground and drives his right fist at your head. This is checked with an upward and outward sweep of your left arm. As this second defensive sweep of your left arm tends to straighten him drive your right fist into his stomach or groin, stepping in with your right foot as you do so.

Movement 2

The attack is warded-off as in Movement 1. As the result of two successive attacks from his right foot and arm he should have his right leg well advanced. Take advantage of this by pointing the toes of your right foot downwards and driving your right knee upwards and forwards into his groin.

Movement 3

Ward-off the right-footed kick with a downwards and outwards sweep of your left arm. The punch to the head

with the opponent's right arm is warded-off with an upwards and outwards blow with your left arm. Do not step in with your left foot. This double attack from your opponent's right side leaves him turned to his left—thus providing the opportunity for a counter from your right side. Immediately take advantage of this and by kicking upwards and forwards drive your right instep up into his groin (Fig. 70).

Fig. 70

Attack 12

This time you are attacked with a kick to the groin with the opponent's left foot followed up with a left-handed punch to your head or upper body.

Movement 1

Ward-off the kick by sweeping your right arm downwards and outwards, thus taking the attack safely past your right side. The follow-up attack with the left fist is warded-away by sweeping your right arm upwards and outwards. To counter use your left arm, which has not taken part in the defence, to drive your left fist into his groin or middle body, stepping forward with the left foot as you do so.

Movement 2

As in Movement 1 ward-off the kick with an outwards and downwards sweep of your right arm, stepping in with your right foot as you do so. Counter the punch to your head with an upwards and outwards sweep of your right arm. Now, pointing the toes of your left foot downwards, drive your left knee forwards and upwards into his groin.

Movement 3

Again the attacks of the opponent's left foot and fist are warded-off as in Movement 1 with successive sweeps of your right arm, but do not step in with your right foot as you defend yourself. Instead use the distance between you to drive your left foot forwards and upwards to deliver a kick with your instep to his groin.

13. Dealing with Kicks and Blows from the Knee

In the previous chapter I introduced defence against the kick. A kick together with an attack with the knee always appears to me to be a form of attack which is far more frightening than the danger resulting from it really merits. These attacks are almost always made to the groin or stomach and should they land there is no doubt that the victim would be disabled and at the mercy of his opponent. However, as the target is the front of the body it is not difficult to ward-off such an attack by a simple twist of the hips. The blow, even should the ward-off fail, will land comparatively harmlessly in the hip area.

It will be noticed that, almost without exception, throughout this book the defender meets the attack by stepping in or stepping back as he wards-off the blow. This automatically turns the body sideways and presents the far less vulnerable side of the body to the attacker. In addition I have constantly emphasised that all movements commence from the Basic Posture and you must return to this posture on completion of each movement. This ensures that as well as having turned the side of the body to the attacker you also have the hand not in use free and well positioned to deal with a kick or drive of the knee to your body.

In the earlier chapters you will have seen how as a rule you use the left arm to ward-off a right-handed blow and the right to ward-off a blow with the left hand. If these attacks are successive your left hand returns to the position of the Basic Posture at your left hip as you ward-off the second attack with your right arm. This is very important as failure to return to the Basic Posture can leave you open to subsequent attacks.

In this chapter I will deal with methods of warding-off and countering kicks and blows with the knee. As one or two of these movements have been included in series already described they should be treated as revision.

Attack 1

Your opponent attacks by kicking to your groin with his right foot. From the Basic Posture take your left fist across your body to the vicinity of the right side of your chest and sweep downwards and outwards to your left to ward-off the kick. Make contact with the fist or edge of the hand, whichever you consider more effective. As you take your left arm across your body advance your left foot so that your left hip faces the kick. Should your defensive sweep with your left arm fail, the kick will then only strike your hip or thigh. As your sweep succeeds return to the Basic Posture. The sweep is aimed at the inside calf of the leg or the inside thigh, depending on how close you are to the opponent. Either blow will cause severe pain should it land on its target.

Attack 2

You are attacked with a left-footed kick to your groin. Stepping forward with your right foot take your right fist up to the vicinity of your left chest and then drive the arm downwards and outwards, sweeping the leg away past your right side with either a hammer-fist or side-hand blow. Return to the Basic Posture.

Fig. 71

Attack 3

This time the attacker drives his right knee upwards and

forwards into your groin. It is impossible to sweep this form of attack away with an arm so your own leg has to be used. As the attack is delivered move your left leg forward and, bending your leg at the knee, drive the knee to your right (Fig. 71) so that it strikes the outside of the attacker's knee or thigh. Not only will this defence succeed in protecting you but it may also disable the opponent's leg. Resume the Basic Posture.

Attack 4

You are attacked by your opponent's left knee which he attempts to drive into your groin. At once advance your right foot and bending the knee drive your own right knee across your body to contact the outside of the attacking knee or thigh. Resume the Basic Posture.

Attack 5

The attacker kicks with his right foot to your groin. At once raise your left leg and bending your left knee drive

Fig. 72

the outside of your left foot down against the lower part of the attacker's shin as he kicks upwards (Fig. 72). This not only checks the attack completely but is in itself a disabling blow. Return to the Basic Posture. Made with a bare foot this block may do no more than ward-off the attack but when performed with the edge of the shoe or boot it is a very effective counter-attack.

Attack 6
The attacker aims a left-foot kick to your groin. Raise your right foot and bending your right knee drive the outside of your foot down against the opponent's shin as he kicks upwards. At once return to the Basic Posture.

Although several of the defensive movements just described are in themselves effective counters you should not rely on them to disable the opponent and so put a second attack against you out of the question. You must therefore at once deliver a decisive counter-attack. The following attacks repeat those already described in this chapter, adding the counters.

Attack 7
The opponent kicks to your groin with his right foot.

Movement 1
Advance your left leg, sweeping the attacking leg downwards and outwards with your left arm as in Attack 1 of this chapter. Now counter-attack by kicking forwards and upwards to his groin with your right foot, making contact with your instep. Return to the Basic Posture.

Movement 2
Against the same attack, the right-footed kick to your groin, step in with your left foot, sweeping outwards and downwards with your left arm. This time as you sweep away the attacking leg slide your left hand under his leg and lift his leg outwards and upwards so stretching his legs outwards (Fig 73). At once drive your right foot upwards and forwards into his groin which is now fully exposed to your kick. Return to the Basic Posture.

Fig. 73

Attack 8
The attacker aims a left-foot kick to your groin.

Movement 1
Step forward with your right foot, sweeping outwards and downwards with your right arm to ward-off the attack. At once counter with a left-foot kick to your opponent's groin and then resume the Basic Posture.

Movement 2
Again you are attacked with a left-foot kick to the groin which is warded-off by stepping forward with the right foot and sweeping outwards and downwards with the right arm. This time as you ward-off slide your right hand under the attacker's left leg and lift it upwards and outwards thus spreading him out so that he is really open to a counter-kick to his groin with your left foot. Resume the Basic Posture.

Attack 9
The opponent attempts to drive his right knee to your groin.

Movement 1

This attack is warded-off by bending the left leg and driving your left knee upwards and across your body so that your knee makes contact with the outside of his right knee or thigh. At once repeat or continue the drive of your left knee into the base of his spine or right side (Fig. 74). Resume the Basic Posture.

Fig. 74

Movement 2

As in Movement 1 ward-off an attack to your groin with your opponent's right knee by bending your own left knee and driving it across your body into the outside of the attacker's knee or thigh. At once replace your left foot on the ground and counter-attack by driving your right knee upwards and forwards into the opponent's groin, stomach or left side. Resume the Basic Posture.

Attack 10

Your attacker attempts to drive his left knee into your groin or stomach.

Movement 1

Bend your right leg and drive the knee across your body into the outside of his knee or thigh. Without a break in your movement continue the drive of your knee upwards or repeat the drive upwards into his left side or the base of his spine. Return to the Basic Posture.

Movement 2

You are attacked by the opponent's left knee which is aimed at your groin or stomach. Defend by bending your right leg and driving the knee across your body into the outside of his knee or thigh. At once replace your right foot on the ground and counter by bending your left leg and driving your left knee upwards and forwards into the attacker's groin. Return to the Basic Posture.

Attack 11
The attacker aims a right-footed kick to your groin.

Movement 1
Lift your right foot, warding-off the kick by bending your right knee and driving the outside of your right foot forwards and downwards against his shin as he kicks upwards. As soon as you have made contact with his shin drive your right knee upward into his groin or stomach. Resume the Basic Posture.

Movement 2
Against the same right-footed kick defend by blocking with the outside of your right foot but instead of countering with a counter-blow with your knee to his groin withdraw your right foot and kick upward to his groin making contact with the instep of your right foot. Resume the Basic Posture.

Attack 12
You are attacked with a left-footed kick to your groin.

Movement 1
Meet his kick by bending your left knee and driving the outside of your left foot down and forward against his shin as he kicks upwards. Immediately, ensuring that the toes of your left foot are pointed downwards to add to the power of your movement, bend your left knee fully and drive the knee upwards and forwards into the attacker's groin or stomach. Return to the Basic Posture.

Movement 2
Again meet his left-footed kick by bending your left knee and driving the outside edge of your left foot down onto

his shin as he makes his kick. Immediately you make your contact with his shin withdraw your leg a little and kick upwards to his groin with the left leg, making contact with your instep. Return to the Basic Posture.

Note: Movements such as that shown in Fig. 73 are very likely to throw the attacker onto his back, shoulder or head as well as ward-off the attack. This can be dangerous even when performed on soft mats. Great care must be taken and I consider that to take a judo beginner's course which includes lessons on falling without injury would be well worth while. The balance and posture taught on such a course is also valuable.

14. Repeated or Successive Counter-Attacks

So far we have practised counters against various forms of attack and also against two successive attacks, but have always stopped when we have made one single counter. As you will see if you think about it your single counter may well be checked and you will certainly find your counters being checked when you progress to free practice. Strictly many of the blocks you have been using are in themselves Karate blows and can disable. Typical examples are the upwards and outwards cut to ward-off the punch to the head and body and the thrust to the shin with the outside of the foot which counters a kick. In the former case the sharp outside (little finger) edge of the hand or forearm meets the soft part of the arm and in the latter case you deliver a powerful blow to the shin. Both are extremely painful and capable of disabling an opponent. However, for the purpose of this chapter I propose to assume that these blocks or counter-attacks have not been decisive and describe some of the successive counters which can be used should the first fail to put your attacker out of action.

Attack 1
You are attacked with a right-handed blow to the head or upper body.

Movement 1
As you are attacked ward-off his right arm by sweeping your left arm with the fingers extended upwards and

outwards. As you do so step in with your left foot. Immediately step in with your right foot and bending your right arm drive your right elbow and forearm upwards and forwards into your opponent's face and jaw. The elbow should contact his jaw and your forearm drive against his face (Fig. 75). Take advantage of the fact that the blow from your right elbow will drive his body backwards or make him bend back to avoid it, to bend your left

Fig. 75

knee and drive the knee upwards and forwards into his groin. Resume the Basic Posture.

Note: It is important that each arm is taken back to the Basic Posture after use. In Movement 1 just described you should return the left fist to its Basic Position at your left hip immediately you have warded-off the blow unless you are using it at once in a counter-move such as bringing your left fist down to his head. By returning your arm to the Basic Posture you are better prepared to ward-off a second blow or make a second counter. One arm should always be returning to the Basic Posture at exactly the same speed as the other leaves the Basic Posture to attack.

Movement 2

Again ward-off the right-arm blow to the head or upper body with an upwards and outwards sweep of your left arm, extending the fingers of the hand as you do so and stepping in with your left foot. As in the first movement counter by stepping in with your right foot and bending your arm at the elbow, drive your right forearm and elbow to the opponent's head. Your elbow should make contact

with his jaw and your forearm with his face. Drive your
left fist, which should have been returned to its basic position immediately it had warded-off the initial blow, into
the opponent's right side or stomach. You could of course
at this stage follow up with a drive of your right knee to
his groin. Return to the Basic Posture.

Movement 3

Once more you are attacked with a right-hand blow to
your head or upper body. This time step in with your
right foot and taking your right hand across your body

Fig. 76

until it is close to your left hip sweep the attacker's
blow away with an upwards and outwards sweep of your
right arm with the fingers extended (Fig. 76). This ward-
off will tend to turn the opponent to his left, so make use
of this to step in with your left foot and drive your left
fist into his side or back. Follow up by bending your right
knee, and pointing the toes downward drive your knee
upward into the opponent's middle body or base of his

spine depending on which way his body is turned at this stage (Fig. 77). Resume the Basic Posture.

Fig. 77

Attack 2
Your attacker drives his left fist to your head or upper body.

Movement 1
Ward-off the blow by sweeping upwards and outwards with your right arm, extending the fingers and stepping in with the right foot as you do so. Immediately step in with your left foot and, bending your left arm at the elbow, drive your left elbow to his jaw, the forearm making contact with his face. This attack will bend his body backwards or at least he will lean back in an attempt to avoid it, so at once bend your left leg and pointing the toes drive your right knee forwards and upwards into his groin. Immediately resume the Basic Posture.

Movement 2
Ward-off the left-hand blow to your head with an upwards and outwards sweep of your right arm. Extend your fingers and step in with the right foot as you do this. At once counter-attack by stepping in with your left foot, and bending your left arm at the elbow drive the elbow and forearm upward and forward into his head, contacting his jaw with your elbow and his face with your forearm. With your right fist which was returned to the Basic Posture as soon as the initial blow was warded-off punch to the opponent's left side or stomach. You can now continue the counter-attack by driving your left knee to his groin. Return to the Basic Posture.

Movement 3

Deflect the left-hand punch to the head by stepping in with your left foot, and taking your left fist across your body to your right hip sweep upwards and across to your left. Straighten the fingers as you do so. This will tend to turn the attacker to his right, so take advantage of this to step in with your right foot and drive your right fist into his side or back. Immediately bend your left leg and drive the knee upwards and forwards into the opponent's middle body or the base of his spine according to his position relative to yourself. Resume the Basic Posture.

Attack 3

The attacker punches to your stomach or middle body with his right fist.

Movement 1

Step in with your left foot, and taking your left arm across your body so that the fist is close to your right breast and

straightening the fingers sweep it downwards and outwards, deflecting the blow past your left side. Immediately step in with your right foot and drive your right fist into the attacker's stomach or middle body. This will bring your opponent's body forward, enabling you to raise your left arm, turning the wrist anti-clockwise as you do so, and cut downwards at the back of his neck making contact with the little finger edge of the left hand (Fig. 78). An alternative is to clench the left fist and deliver a hammer-fist blow with the little finger edge of the fist to the back of his head. Resume the Basic Posture.

Fig. 78

Movement 2

Step in with your left foot, warding-off his punch to your middle body with a downwards and outwards sweep of your left arm. The fingers should be extended. To make your sweep, your left fist should first be taken up close to your right breast. Immediately advance your right leg and bending the knee drive your knee upwards and forwards into his groin. Follow up by driving your left fist, which should have been returned to its basic position at your left hip, into the opponent's right side. Return to the Basic Posture.

Movement 3

Ward-off his right-fist punch to your middle body by taking your right fist up to the vicinity of your left breast then, extending the fingers, sweeping downwards and across your body. This sweep wards the blow away past your right side. As you move your arm step in with your right foot. As the blow is warded-off bend your left leg at the knee and pointing your toes downwards drive the knee upwards into the opponent's back or to the base of his spine. This should be easy as the warding-off operation will have turned him to his left. Immediately follow by extending the fingers of your right hand and driving the fingertips upwards and forward into the opponent's throat. At once resume the Basic Posture.

Attack 4

Your opponent attempts to drive his left fist into your middle body.

Movement 1

Ward-off the blow by stepping in with your right foot and taking your right arm up across your body so that the fist is close to your left breast, extend the fingers and sweep downwards and across your body. The blow is thus swept past your right side. Immediately step in with your left foot and drive your left fist into the attacker's stomach or middle body. This counter will have the effect

of bending the opponent forward, so take advantage of
this by raising your right arm and turning the wrist
clockwise, cut downwards at his exposed neck, making
contact with the back of his neck with the little finger
edge of your right hand. A hammer-fist blow to the back
of his head or neck with the little finger edge of the right
fist would be equally efficient. Return to the Basic Posture.

Movement 2

Ward-off the left-hand punch by stepping in with your
right foot and taking your right fist close to your left
breast, extend the fingers and sweep downwards and to
your right. At once advance your left leg and bending
the knee drive it forward and upward into the attacker's
groin. Without any delay make a second counter-attack
by driving your right fist which you have taken back to
its Basic Posture into his left side or stomach. Resume the
Basic Posture.

Movement 3

Again we have the left-hand blow aimed at your middle
body but this time ward it off with your left arm. To do
this take your left fist up to your right breast and extending the fingers sweep downwards and outwards, guiding
the opponent's punch past your left side. To do this you
must step in with your left foot as you commence the
defensive move. As you successfully ward-off the blow
bend your right leg at the knee and pointing your toes
downwards drive the knee upwards and forwards into the
opponent's back or the base of his spine, which will have
been turned towards you by your warding-off action.
Without delay follow up by extending the fingers of your
left hand and driving them into his throat. Resume the
Basic Posture.

15. Defence and Counter-Attack by Stepping Back

So far you have been stepping in towards your opponent as part of your initial defensive action. As I have already explained this has several advantages. It turns your body so that you present your side to him. It brings you inside his arms, so making it difficult for him to have room to make a second attack; it also brings you close enough to deliver your own counter-blows.

Against this must be set the obvious disadvantage that it brings you close to an opponent who may be able to grab you and, should he have superior strength, will then overwhelm you. In addition it must be remembered that one of the great assets of the Karateman is his ability to use his feet as a result of his training. Any practised Karateman should be able to kick forward to the head of an average height opponent, and not far short of this to the side. The power and effectiveness of these kicks can only be used when there is sufficient space between the Karateman and his attacker. To provide this space it is necessary to step or move away from the opponent as his attack is warded-off. This movement of course also turns the side of the body toward the attacker. This chapter commences with foot movements only, beginning and ending in the Basic Posture. The hands are held in the Basic Posture throughout each movement.

Movement 1

From the Basic Posture step back with the right foot. The movement is a gliding of the foot across the ground. The foot should not be picked up and banged down when withdrawn. The weight of the body should be distributed equally between the feet at the conclusion of the movement (Fig. 79). This places you in a position to counter equally well with either foot. Now withdraw the left foot to resume the Basic Posture.

Movement 2

From the Basic Posture withdraw the left foot in a gliding movement along the ground. As the foot is replaced on the ground the weight should be equally distributed between the feet. Fig. 79 shows this but with the other

Fig. 79   Fig. 80   Fig. 81

foot taken back. In this position you can counter equally well with either foot. Withdraw the right foot and return to the Basic Posture.

Movement 3

From the Basic Posture step back with the right foot, gliding it along the floor. At the end of the movement, place the weight over the left foot. The right foot should be allowed to rest on the ground but lightly so that it can be brought into action immediately in a counter-attack (Fig. 80). Now recover your right foot, advancing it to return to the Basic Posture.

Movement 4

From the Basic Posture step back with the left foot,

gliding it along the ground but maintaining the weight of the body on the right foot. In this position you are better prepared to counter-attack with the left foot. Fig. 80 shows this position but with the feet reversed. Now recover your Basic Posture by advancing the left foot to its original position.

Movement 5

From the Basic Posture step back with the right foot, placing your weight upon it immediately (Fig. 81). This puts you in a good position to counter-attack with the left foot. Now withdraw your left foot to resume the Basic Posture.

Movement 6

From the Basic Posture take back the left foot, placing the weight on that foot as soon as it is replaced on the ground. (See Fig. 81, in which the feet are reversed.) In this position it is possible to counter-attack rapidly with the right foot. Now return to the Basic Posture by withdrawing the right foot.

At this stage these six movements should be repeated time after time until they can be made rapidly and smoothly. It is pointless to continue with the counter-kicks until the preliminary defensive movement can be made effectively.

Movement 7

Step back with the right foot, allowing your weight to be distributed equally between the feet. This position allows you to use either foot as a counter-attacking weapon. At once transfer your weight and balance to the right foot and kick forwards and upwards with your left foot. Withdraw the left foot to return to the Basic Posture.

Movement 8

Again step back with the right foot, placing the weight equally between the feet. This time transfer the weight and balance to the left foot and kick forward and upwards with the right foot. Return to the Basic Posture on returning the right foot to the ground.

Movement 9

Step back with the left foot, allowing your weight to be distributed equally between your feet as you replace it on the ground. Immediately transfer your weight to your left foot and kick upwards and forwards with your right. Replace your right foot on the ground, resuming the Basic Posture.

Movement 10

Again step back with the left foot, returning it to the ground with the weight distributed equally between the feet. At once transfer the weight to the right foot and kick forwards and upwards with the left. Return to the Basic Posture as you return the left foot to the floor.

Movement 11

Step back with the right foot, keeping the weight and balance on the left. The right foot should be in contact with the ground, but with no weight upon it you can at once kick forwards and upwards. As you bring the right foot down from the kick, return to the Basic Posture.

Movement 12

Step back with the left foot, retaining the weight and balance on the right foot as you do so. At once kick forwards and upwards with the left foot, returning to the Basic Posture as you bring it to the ground.

Movement 13

Step back with the right foot, at once placing the weight and balance upon it. At once bring your left foot back in order to retain your balance and kick forwards and upwards with it. As you lower the foot from the kick, return to the Basic Posture.

Movement 14

Step back with the left foot, immediately placing your weight and balance upon it. Take your right foot back in order to retain your balance and kick forwards and upwards with it. As you lower the foot from the kick, return to the Basic Posture.

16. Counters to Attacks to the Head

IN this chapter I continue to describe Karate movements which incorporate withdrawing from the attack but this time I commence each movement with the defence against various attacks and then continue with the counter-attack.

Attack 1
You are attacked by an opponent who aims a right-handed punch at your head or upper body.

Movement 1
Ward-off the blow with an upwards and outwards sweep of the left arm. The fingers are kept straight and contact made with the little finger edge of the forearm, wrist or hand. At the same time step back with the right foot, distributing your weight equally between the feet. The delivery of a right-handed blow will normally turn the opponent a little to his left, exposing the front of his body to your right foot. Make use of this to transfer your balance to the left foot and kick upwards and forwards with the right. This kick should be aimed at the opponent's groin or stomach. If you have the ability, the kick can be aimed at the head. Replace the right foot on the ground and take back your left foot to return to the Basic Posture.

Movement 2
Ward-off the blow with the same upwards and outwards sweep of the left arm, withdrawing the right foot as you do so. The weight is distributed equally between your

feet. At once transfer your weight and balance to the right foot and, taking the left hip and leg back to provide the necessary space between you and the opponent, kick upwards and forwards to his right side. This is possible because his right-hand punch turns him to his left. Take the left foot back, replacing it on the ground so that you are once more in the Basic Posture.

Movement 3

Ward-off the blow with an upwards and forwards sweep of the left arm, moving your right foot back as you do so. This time although the right foot is placed on the ground no weight is transferred to it. Immediately swing the foot forward once more delivering a kick to the front of the opponent's body making the groin, stomach or head the target. Replace the foot on the ground so that you are again in the Basic Posture.

Movement 4

Ward-off the blow with an upwards and forwards sweep of the left hand, again stepping back with the right foot, to which you transfer your weight and balance. At once bring the left hip and leg back and deliver a left-footed kick to the opponent's right side. This would be turned towards you as a result of his blow. Now replace your left foot on the ground so that you are in the Basic Posture.

Movement 5

Sweep away the blow by warding-off outwards and upwards with the left arm, stepping back and to your right with the right foot (Fig. 82) but without placing your weight and balance upon it. At once kick forward with the right foot, aiming at the front of his body. The target should be the groin, stomach or head. He may have turned sufficiently to make the target the right side of his body.

Movement 6

This is exactly the same as in Movement 5, the left-hand

Fig. 82

defensive sweep but this time step back and to the right
with the right foot whilst your balance is transferred to the
right foot. At once with-
draw your left foot and
achieve a left-foot kick to
the front or right side of
the opponent's body. Re-
turn to the Basic Posture.

Fig. 83

Movement.7

As the attack is made ward-
off the blow with an up-
wards and outwards sweep
of the left hand. At the same
time step back and to your
left with your right foot
(Fig. 83). Transfer your
weight and balance to your
right foot and kick for-
ward and upwards to the
attacker's side or back
with your left foot. Replace your left foot on the mat and
advance your right foot to return to the Basic Posture.

Attack 2

Your opponent aims a left-handed blow to your head or upper body.

Movement 1

Ward-off the blow with an upwards and outwards sweep of your right arm. The fingers should be straightened and contact made with the little finger edge of the hand, wrist or forearm. As you ward-off step back with the left foot so that your weight is equally divided between your feet. With your weight equally distributed it is possible to use either foot as a counter-weapon. However, as a left-handed blow will most likely turn your opponent a little to his right, so exposing the front of his body to a left-foot kick, transfer your weight to your right foot and kick upwards and forwards with your left. The target should be the opponent's groin, stomach or head. Replace the left foot on the mat and resume the Basic Posture by moving your right foot back.

Movement 2

Again you ward-off his left-hand punch with an upward sweep of the right arm. Your fingers should be extended and the contact made with the little finger edge. As you make your defensive sweep, withdraw your left foot, distributing your weight equally between both feet. Follow this immediately by transferring your balance to your left foot, taking the right hip and foot back in order to provide sufficient space between you and your opponent to enable you to counter-attack. As his left-hand punch will no doubt have turned him to his right take the opportunity offered to kick with your right foot upwards and forwards to his left side. Now withdraw your left foot so that you resume the Basic Posture.

Movement 3

Ward-off the attack with an upwards and outwards sweep of your right arm, fingers extended and contacting with the little finger side. Your left foot is moved back but your weight is left completely on your right foot so leaving the left free to kick. At once deliver a left-footed kick to the front of the opponent's body aiming at the groin, stomach or head. Return the foot to the ground, regaining the Basic Posture.

Movement 4

Ward-off the blow with an upwards and outwards sweep of the right hand, stepping back with the left foot and transferring all your weight on to it. Immediately take back the right hip and leg and drive the foot forwards and upwards to the opponent's left side, which has been turned towards you as a result of his punch. It is important to withdraw the right hip and leg before the kick is delivered in order to provide space for it. Your right foot should be replaced on the ground in order to resume the Basic Posture.

Movement 5

The left-handed punch to the head is warded-off with an upwards and outwards sweep of the right arm, fingers extended, making contact with the little finger edge. At the same time step back and to your left with the left foot but do not place your weight and balance upon it. Without any break in your movement swing the left foot forward again and upwards thus kicking to the front of his body and making contact with his groin, stomach or head. Fig. 82 shows the foot movement but with the feet and arms reversed. Return the left foot to the ground to resume the Basic Posture. Should the opponent have turned into a suitable position as he punched, the kick could be aimed at the side of his body.

Movement 6

The left-handed punch is warded-off in exactly the same way as in Movement 5 above, and again the left foot is taken back to the left, but this time the weight and balance are transferred to it. Immediately withdraw the right hip and leg and kick forward and upward with the right foot to the left side or front of the opponent's body. Resume the Basic Posture.

Movement 7

As the left-hand punch is made, ward it off with an up-

wards and outwards sweep of the right hand, at the same
time stepping back and to the right with the left foot.
Fig. 83 shows this with right and left reversed. As you

Fig. 84

step back transfer your weight and balance to the left
foot and kick forwards and upwards to the attacker's
back with the right foot. Replace the right foot on the
ground and advance the left to return to the Basic
Posture.

Note: Throughout this chapter I have stated that the
target for the counter-attacking kick is the middle of the
body or the head. Whilst the expert in Karate may well
be able to reach the head with his kick it is very unlikely
indeed that the reader will be able to do so and as any
effort to over-reach will certainly result in the loss of the
balance to the rear it is unwise to attempt anything too
ambitious. As soon as an attempt is made to over-
stretch upwards all power leaves the kick and this
counter can be very successfully counter-attacked in its
turn. It is wise to attempt only what is possible to you,
and so my advice is restrict the counters to kicks to the
middle of the body or the side which is turned towards
you.

17. Counters to Attacks to the Middle Body by Stepping Back

THIS chapter deals with more counter-attacks in which you defend by stepping back. In this case the attacks are made to the middle body. I think you will find from experience that to step back as you ward-off such an attack tends to leave all your weight and balance on the front foot, especially when warding-off downwards. That is the foot which you have not moved. In Karate, as in all forms of self-defence, it is a fatal mistake to attempt any movement which does not come easily and naturally to you; to do so will only result in a slow and cumbersome movement which must be ineffective. Do not worry about this as a little practice will enable you to move smoothly backwards whilst warding-off the attack and enable you to distribute your balance as you consider most effective.

Movement 1
Sweep downwards and outwards with the left arm, first taking the left fist from the Basic Posture at the hip up to the vicinity of the right breast. As the sweep is made, take back the right foot, placing it on the ground but leaving all your weight and balance on the left foot. Advance the right foot to resume the Basic Posture.

Movement 2
Sweep downwards and outwards with the left arm as in Movement 1 above at the same time taking the right foot back. This time the weight and balance are at once

127

distributed equally between the feet. Step forward with the right foot returning to the Basic Posture.

Movement 3

Once more defend by raising the left hand to the right of the chest and sweeping downwards and outwards. At the same time step back with the right foot placing the weight and balance upon it immediately it touches the floor. Move the right foot forward in order to resume the Basic Posture.

Movement 4

Raise the right fist from its basic position at your right hip to the vicinity of the left breast at once sweeping downwards and outwards. Simultaneously step back with the left foot leaving your weight and balance on the right foot as you do so. Return the left foot to its original position resuming the Basic Posture.

Movement 5

Again raise the right fist to the left of the chest and sweep downwards and outwards, at the same time stepping back with the left foot placing your weight and balance equally on both feet as the left is placed on the ground. The left foot is advanced to resume the Basic Posture.

Movement 6

Taking the right fist close to the left breast or shoulder, sweep downwards and outwards with it. Simultaneously step back with the left foot, immediately transferring your weight and balance to it as you do so. To resume the Basic Posture advance the left leg to its original position.

Note: It should be noted that in almost all the movements described and practised so far the left foot has been advanced as the defensive sweep has been made with the left arm and the right foot advanced with a right-arm sweep. Similarly, the right foot has been taken back with a left-arm sweep and of course the left foot when the right arm sweeps. Most people find that this is the natural movement but there is no physical reason why the right

foot should not be advanced as a defensive sweep is made
with the left arm. However, for tactical reasons this is not
a sound principle upon which a beginner should base
his self-defence.

Should you be attacked with a right-hand punch to the
head or upper body the attacker normally steps forward
with his right foot. He must do this if he is to develop a
reasonable amount of power. Equally he must place his
weight upon his right foot to punch effectively. The
defender on the other hand by warding-off with the left

Fig. 85

arm and advancing his left leg turns his left side to the
attacker and leaves his right arm free to defend his body
(Fig. 84) from a second attack made with the left arm or
leg (Fig. 85). In addition he has his right arm and leg
free to counter-attack an opponent who has the vulnerable front of his body exposed.

Now take the case of a defence against a right-hand
punch made by warding-off with the left arm whilst
stepping in with the right leg (Fig. 86). The defender's
body is exposed to a second attack made with the right
foot or knee whilst his own right arm and leg are not so
well positioned for a counter-attack. They are too close

to the opponent and not in a good position to attack any part of the body as his balance is on the right foot.

If on the other hand a right-handed punch is warded-off with a sweep of the right hand the right foot is advanced. This exposes the attacker's right side to your counter-attack (Fig. 87), and leaves the defender fairly safe against a left-handed second attack.

Fig. 86

The remainder of this chapter deals with counter-attack following up the defences practised in the movements already described. Whilst practising these defences and counters it will be profitable to consider the points I have made in the preceding paragraphs.

Attack 1

The attacker punches at the middle of your body with his right hand.

Movement 1

Defend by warding-off with an outwards and downwards sweep of the left arm, first having taken the fist up to the area of the right shoulder. The fingers may be extended and contact made with the little finger edge of the hand or forearm or equally well a hammer-fist blow can be used.

As you sweep take back the right foot, retaining your weight and balance on your left as you do so. Immediately counter by kicking forwards and upwards at the opponent's groin, stomach or knee with the right foot which is free for this purpose as no weight has been placed upon it. Resume the Basic Posture as you return the right foot to the mat.

Fig. 87

Movement 2
Defend in the manner described in Movement 1 using a downwards and outwards sweep of the left arm. As you step back with the right foot, distribute your weight and balance equally between your feet. From this position you can either kick upwards to the front of the opponent's body with the right foot or kick to the side of the body with the left foot. Return to the Basic Posture.

Movement 3
Again the defence is the downwards and outwards sweep of the left arm. As you sweep step back with the right foot, place all your weight and balance upon it as you put it on the ground. Immediately take the left foot off the ground and withdraw the hip using the space so

provided between you and your opponent to kick upwards and forwards to the right side of his body. Return to the Basic Posture.

Movement 4

This time the opponent's right-hand punch to the middle body is warded-off with a downward sweep of the right hand made across the body from left to right. It starts in the vicinity of the left shoulder. Simultaneously step back with the left foot leaving your weight and balance on your right foot as you do so. Immediately withdraw your left hip taking your left foot off the mat and kick upwards and forwards to the opponent's back. Return to the Basic Posture.

Attack 2

The opponent attacks to your middle body with a left-hand punch.

Movement 1

The defence is made with the right arm, sweeping it downwards and outwards from the area of the left shoulder. The fingers should be extended and contact made with the little finger edge of the hand or forearm, or a hammerfist blow may be used. At the same time withdraw the left foot, maintaining your weight and balance on your right foot as you do so. Immediately counter-attack with an upwards and forwards kick with the left foot aiming at the opponent's groin, stomach or head. Return your right foot to the mat to resume the Basic Posture.

Movement 2

The same defence is used, the outwards and downwards sweep of the right hand. Simultaneously withdraw the left foot, placing your weight and balance equally on both feet as you return it to the mat. This enables you to counter with either foot as convenient. With the left foot you can kick upwards and forwards to the front of the opponent's body or with the right foot kick upwards to the side of his body. Resume the Basic Posture.

Movement 3

Defend with a downwards and outwards sweep of the right arm, at the same time stepping back with the left foot, immediately placing all your weight and balance upon it. At once take the right foot off the ground and withdraw the right hip taking the leg with it. Use the space provided by this move to kick upwards and forwards to the left side of his body. Resume the Basic Posture.

Movement 4

Ward-off the left-hand punch to the middle body with a downward sweep of the left arm made across the body from the right to the left. At the same time step back with the right foot, leaving all your weight and balance on your left. Immediately withdraw your right hip and kick upwards and forwards with it to the opponent's back. Return to the Basic Posture.

18. Defence against Kicks by Stepping Back

IT is just as easy to defend against kicks by stepping back as it is against blows with the fist. In fact as the leg is a longer and more powerful weapon it may well be better to do so. For the same reason kicks are not always warded-off by Karatemen with sweeps of the arms. Instead a cross-arm defence is used. From the Basic Posture the defender moves both arms inwards so that they cross in front of him and block the kick with the "V" formed between them. Contact is made with the little finger edges of the forearms. The position is shown in Fig. 88. This is a solid block although by turning the hips the body may be turned so deflecting the attacker's leg to the left (Fig. 89) or the right, thus making the defence safer and more effective.

Fig. 88

Although kicks are warded-off with sweeps of the arms (unless the cross-arm defence is used) in exactly the same manner as the blows were checked in the last chapter, Chapter 17, there are differences in the counters. This is because whilst delivering a punch turns the attacker sideways (Fig. 90) an attack with a kick does not usually do so (Fig. 91). Instead of leaving the side of the body open to counter it opens up the front of the body particularly to a kick (Fig. 91). As, therefore, you require a certain amount of space to deliver a kick the stepping-back method of defence is particularly appropriate.

134

Fig. 89

Fig. 90

It should be remembered that whilst a powerful sweep to the soft underside of the attacker's forearm with the edge of the hand or forearm is very likely to disable the attacker, a similar sweep made against the leg which

Fig. 91

kicks at you is far less likely to succeed in doing so. The leg is so much more powerful than the arm that although a strong, accurate sweep to the inside of the calf of the leg may be very painful it is unlikely to have much more effect than that of warding-off the attack. This of course is important in itself, but it is more important to remember that the wider and farther the leg is swept outwards the more likely it is to deflect the kick and the more it opens up the front of the attacker's body to a counter-attack. It may well be considered better to use a hammer-fist blow when sweeping away a kick than an open-hand cut.

Attack 1
The attacker, facing you, aims a forward and upward kick to your groin or stomach with his right foot.

Movement 1
Deflect the kick away to your left with a downward and

outward sweep of your left arm. The fist is first taken close
to the right shoulder and then swept down with fingers
extended making contact with the little finger edge of the
hand or forearm or with the little finger edge of the fist
if a hammer-fist blow is used. Sweep well away to the
left so that by taking the leg outwards his legs are well
separated. As the defensive sweep is made step back with
the right foot, leaving the weight and balance fully on the
left foot (Fig. 92). Without any break in the movement,

Fig. 92

at once kick forwards and upwards with the right foot,
stretching forward the toes so that your instep is driven
upwards into his groin (Fig. 93). Replace the right foot
on the ground resuming the Basic Posture.

Movement 2
Ward-off the kick with an outwards and downwards sweep
of the left arm, first taking the fist from its basic position
at the left hip up to the vicinity of the right breast or
shoulder. Again ward outwards very powerfully in order
to take the kicking leg well to your left. As you ward-off
step back with the right foot distributing the weight and
balance equally between the feet as you replace the right
foot on the ground. At this stage you can kick upwards

and forwards to the groin with the instep of the right
foot as in Movement 1 or, alternatively, take the left foot
off the ground and withdrawing the left hip and the left
leg kick upwards with it to the opponent's groin. As the

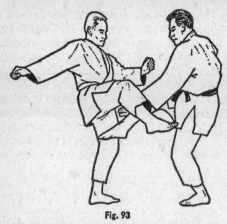

Fig. 93

left-foot kick from this position may well be checked by
the front of the shin meeting the underside of his right
thigh this kick should be made with the toes and not the
instep. Resume the Basic Posture.

Note: There is no doubt that placing the weight equally
on both feet slows down the counter which follows.
This is because before the kick can be made with the right
foot the balance has to be transferred to the left and of
course transferred to the right when the kick is made
with the left foot. Against this must be set the advantage
gained by the freedom to counter with either leg as
circumstances demand.

Movement 3

Ward-off the kick with a downwards and outwards sweep
of the left arm, taking the right foot back as you do so
and immediately transferring the weight and balance to
that right foot as it is placed on the ground. Without
any break in the movement withdraw the left hip and

leg and kick upwards with the toe to the opponent's groin. Finally return to the Basic Posture.

Movement 4

This time the right-footed kick is warded-off with a downwards and outwards sweep of the right hand and arm. The fist is first taken from the basic position at the right hip to the vicinity of the left shoulder and then with fingers extended sweep across, contact being made with the little finger edge of the hand or forearm. Equally well the hammer-fist blow may be used. At the same time the left leg is taken back, the weight and balance being retained on the right foot, which does not move. Immediately the left foot kicks upwards and forwards to the opponent's groin, contact being made with your toes. Return to the Basic Posture.

Movement 5

For the first time you use the cross-arm defence. As the opponent kicks with his right foot your right fist is taken across your body to your left and your left fist across to your right so that your arms cross in front of your body (Fig. 88). The cross is made at about the middle of the forearms. The fists remain lightly clenched to avoid the danger of the fingers being damaged by the kick and the arms are held so that the palms are facing downwards. The arms are held sufficiently in front of you to allow the arms to give to the blow, but still make the defence effective. The kick is now caught or blocked in the "V" formed by your arms as soon as possible, whilst at the same time you take your right foot back, leaving your weight and balance on the left foot. At once use the free right foot to kick upwards and forwards to the attacker's groin. If the attacker's kick has been warded-away a little to the left the toes should be pointed and the kick delivered with the instep. If the block is made in front of the body or to the right this may not be possible and the toes should be used (Fig. 94). Return to the Basic Posture.

Attack 2

Your opponent attacks by kicking forward and upward to your groin with his left foot.

Fig. 94

Movement 1

Deflect the kick away to your right with a downward and outward sweep of your right arm. The fist is first carried up close to the left shoulder and then swept down with fingers extended to make contact with the little finger edge of the hand or forearm or alternatively the little finger edge of the right fist. Sweep away well to the right to separate his legs for your counter-kick. As the kick is swept away step back with the left foot, leaving your weight and balance fully on the right foot. Without any hesitation kick forwards and upwards with the left foot, aiming at the opponent's groin which should be fully exposed by your warding-off action. Stretch the toes of the kicking foot forward so that contact is made with the instep. Replace the left foot on the mat, returning to the Basic Posture.

Movement 2

Ward-off the opponent's kick with an outwards and downwards sweep of the right arm, having first taken it up to the left shoulder. The fingers should be extended and contact made with the little finger edge of the hand or forearm or a hammer-fist blow could be used. At the same time step back with the left foot, placing your weight equally on both feet. This enables you to use either foot for your counter-attack as you wish or as the opportunity arises.

With the left foot, which has been taken back, you kick forward and upwards to the groin using the instep to make contact. For the right foot you must take the hip and foot back to give you room to move and then kick upwards and forwards to the groin using the toes instead of the instep. This is necessitated because the front of your shin may well be blocked by the underside of the opponent's thigh if an attempt is made to use the instep. Return to the Basic Posture.

Movement 3

Ward-off the kick with a downwards and outwards sweep of the right arm using your hand or fist, first taking the hand close to the left shoulder in order to obtain momentum. At the same time step back with the left foot, immediately transferring all your weight and balance to it. Without breaking your movement withdraw your right hip and leg and then kick forwards and upwards with it, aiming your toes at the opponent's groin. Return to the Basic Posture.

Movement 4

Ward-off the attacker's left-footed kick with a powerful downwards and outwards sweep of the left hand and arm, first having taken the fist up to the area of your right shoulder. As usual extend the fingers and make contact with the little finger edge of the hand or arm unless you decide to make a hammer-fist attack. Simultaneously the right leg is taken back, the weight and balance being placed on the left foot, which is not moved. Without placing the right foot on the ground kick forward and upward with it to the opponent's groin using the toes to make contact. Resume the Basic Posture.

Movement 5

This time the cross-arm defence is used. It does not

matter which foot is used by your opponent to attack you, the block being made in the same way. Take the fists and arms across the body so that they are crossed in front of you. They actually cross about half-way down the forearms. It does not matter which arm is placed on top if you are going to counter with a leg. If, however, the counter-attack is to be made with an arm it must be remembered that only the top arm can be used effectively, as the lower arm may be held too low down to be used effectively for a counter-punch.

Block the opponent's left-foot kick with the cross-arm defence, at the same time taking back the left foot, leaving the weight and balance on the right. Fig. 94 shows this but with right and left reversed. At once kick upwards and forwards to the attacker's groin with the left foot. Use the toes if the kick has been blocked away to the left or directly to the front and the instep if the attack has been blocked to the right. Return to the Basic Posture.

19. The Cross-Arm Defence

IN Chapter 18 I introduced the "cross-arm" defence. In my examples this form of block was used against a kick but it is just as effective against a blow. Three points must be borne in mind when defending in this manner:

1. When blocking a downward blow do not block it straight in front of you. If you do so you will find that the flexibility of the wrist will allow any weapon held by the attacker to carry on and hit your head. Should the block be made slightly to left or right there will be no danger of this so the defence will be successful.

2. If the attack against which this defence is used is a straight punch to the head or upper body remember that to cross the arms to block the blow will be ineffective. The fist will drive straight between the arms. To make it effective the block must deflect the blow upward over the defender's head or to his left or right.

3. Do not cross the arms so that the cross is too close to your own body. A kick develops considerable power and you must expect your arms to give way to a fair extent. In fact you may damage your arms if they do not give at all. The arms should be held so that the cross of the arms is about two feet in front of the body. This allows them to give a little, rather like shock absorbers, without the kick reaching your body.

Attack 1

The opponent aims a downward blow at your head with his right arm. No doubt he will be holding a weapon, such as a stick.

Fig. 95

Movement 1

Ward-off the blow by taking the arms upwards and across the body, keeping the fists lightly clenched. In this case your right arm is kept on top. The blow is warded off to your left side so that the weapon will miss your head should it carry on (Fig. 95). As the blow is safely avoided drive your right fist sideways and downwards to the opponent's neck or side of his head. As the blow is blocked to the left you should step forward with the left foot. Take it back to return to the Basic Posture.

Movement 2

Again ward-off the blow to the left, stepping forward with the left foot, using the cross-arm defence this time with the left arm on top. Immediately drive your right elbow or forearm to the opponent's face. Take back the left foot to resume the Basic Posture.

Movement 3

Again the downward blow to the head with the right arm blocked with the cross-arm defence, but this time to the right, stepping in with the right foot as you do this. The arms are crossed with the left arm on top and as the blow is blocked away the left arm is used to deliver a downward or sideways cut with the little finger edge of the hand to the opponent's neck. Alternatively a hammer-fist blow with the little finger edge of the left fist can be delivered to the temple or side of the head. Resume the Basic Posture by withdrawing the right foot.

Movement 4

As for Movement 3 step in with the right foot, blocking the

blow with a cross-arm defence to the right, but this time the right arm on top. From this position it may not be easy to deliver a cut to the neck but instead a hammer-fist blow with the little finger edge of the left fist can be made to the opponent's jaw. Step back with the right foot to resume the Basic Posture.

Attack 2

The attack is a downward blow to the head with the left hand. No doubt a weapon will be used.

Movement 1

Ward-off the blow with an upward cross-arm defence which is made to the right of your body. At the same time step in with your right foot. In your block your left arm is placed on top. As the blow is safely blocked slash downwards to the opponent's neck with the little finger edge of the open left hand or use a hammer-fist attack to the temple or side of his head with the left fist. Withdraw the right foot to resume the Basic Posture.

Movement 2

Ward-off the blow to the right, stepping in with the right foot as you do so. Again the cross-arm defence is used, this time with the right arm on top. At once drive your left elbow and forearm to the opponent's jaw or face. Return to the Basic Posture by taking back the right foot.

Movement 3

Ward-off the downward blow to the head with a cross-arm defence to the left, stepping in with the left foot as you do so. In this block the right arm is on top. Immediately use your right arm to cut downwards with the little finger edge of the right hand to the opponent's neck. As an alternative you can drive your right fist to the temple or side of his head. Take back the left foot to resume the Basic Posture.

Movement 4

Once more ward-off the downward blow by stepping in

with the left foot as you block it with a cross-arm defence to the left, placing the left arm on top. At once use the right arm to deliver a hammer-fist blow with the little finger edge of the right fist to the jaw. Step back with the left and resume the Basic Posture.

Attack 3

The attacker attempts to drive his right fist straight into your face or upper body.

Movement 1

Step in with the left foot, warding-off the blow to the left with an upward cross-arm defence to the left. Place the right arm on top as the arms are crossed. From this position use the right fist to drive a hammer-fist blow to the temple or head or an edge of the hand cut to the side of the neck. Take the left foot back to return to the Basic Posture.

Movement 2

Again ward-off the blow with a cross-arm defence to the left, stepping in with the left foot as you do so, but this time the left arm is placed on top as the arms are crossed. As the blow is warded-away drive the right fist to the opponent's stomach or middle body or to his right side if he has been turned to his left as he delivered his attack. Note how the left arm will hold the opponent's right arm away as the counter-blow is delivered. Return to the Basic Posture by stepping back with the left foot.

Movement 3

Once more step in with the left foot, warding the blow upwards over your head. Use the cross-arm defence and this time place the left arm on top. Counter by driving the right elbow to the jaw or driving your right fist into the stomach or middle body, or the side of his body should he have turned. Return to the Basic Posture by withdrawing the left foot.

Movement 4

Defend exactly as in Movement 3 but this time place the

right arm on top. Counter by slashing to the neck with a downward cut with the little finger edge of the right hand, a hammer-fist blow, or by driving the left fist into the right side of the opponent's body. Take back the left foot, returning to the Basic Posture.

Movement 5

Drive the blow upwards with a cross-arm defence, stepping in with the left foot as you do so. Immediately counter by driving the right knee forward and upward to the opponent's groin. Resume the Basic Posture.

Movement 6

This defence is exactly the same as those used in Movements 4 and 5 but this time as the attack is blocked the right foot is driven forwards and upwards to deliver a kick to the opponent's groin or stomach. Return to the Basic Posture.

Movement 7

Block the right-arm blow to the face with a cross-arm defence to the right, stepping in with the right foot as you do so. This time the left arm is on top. At once deliver a hammer-fist attack to the opponent's temple or head with the little finger side of the left fist, or cut to the side of his neck with the little finger edge of the left hand. Withdraw the right foot to return to the Basic Posture.

Movement 8

As in Movement 6 block the blow with the right arm uppermost. Counter by driving the left fist to the opponent's stomach, or right side should his blow have turned him sufficiently. Take back the right foot, resuming the Basic Posture.

Attack 4

Your opponent attacks with a left-handed punch straight to your face or upper body.

Movement 1

Step in with the right foot, warding-off the blow to the

right with an upwards and outwards cross-arm defence, placing the left arm on top as the arms are crossed. At once use the left fist to deliver a hammer-fist counter to the opponent's temple or side of his head or an edge of the hand cut to the side of his neck. Step back with the right foot, returning to the Basic Posture.

Movement 2

Ward-off the blow with a cross-arm defence to the right, stepping in with the right foot as you do so. This time the right arm is placed on top as the arms are crossed. As the blow is warded away drive the left fist to the opponent's stomach or middle body or to his left side if his blow has turned his body sufficiently. Return to the Basic Posture by stepping back with the right foot.

Movement 3

Step in with the right foot, warding the blow upwards above your head. Use the cross-arm defence this time placing the right arm on top. Counter by driving the left elbow to the opponent's jaw or driving your left fist into his stomach or middle body or the side of his body should he have turned. Withdraw your right foot to resume the Basic Posture.

Movement 4

Defend as in Movement 3 but this time with the left arm on top. Counter by cutting to the neck with a downward cut with the little finger edge of the left hand or by driving the right fist into the left side of the opponent's body. Withdraw the right foot to return to the Basic Posture.

Movement 5

Drive the blow upwards with a cross-arm defence, stepping in with the right foot as you do so. Immediately counter by driving the left knee forward and upward to the opponent's groin. Resume the Basic Posture.

Movement 6

This defence is a repeat of those used in Movements 4

and 5 but this time do not step in as the attack is warded-off, the left foot is driven forwards and upwards to the opponent's groin or stomach. Resume the Basic Posture.

Movement 7

Block the left-arm blow to the face with a cross-arm defence to the left, stepping-in with the left foot as you do so. This time the right arm is on top. At once deliver a hammer-fist blow to the opponent's temple or head with the little finger side of the right fist or a cut to the side of the neck with the little finger edge of the right hand. Withdraw the left foot to return to the Basic Posture.

Movement 8

As in Movement 6 block the blow, but with the left arm uppermost. Counter by driving the right fist to the opponent's stomach or left side if this has been exposed to your attack by his original blow. Take back the left foot, returning to the Basic Posture.

Note: As to be effective all defence has to be instinctive, it is obvious that in Karate no thought can be given to placing the left or right hand on top as the blow is blocked. Even the type of counter used cannot be considered, so until you are ·sufficiently practised you will have no idea whether you will ward off with one hand or both. The defence must be automatic as must the counter-attack. The only means of reaching the required proficiency is practice, practice and still more practice.

20. Breaking and Countering Grips on the Wrists

GRIPS on the wrists appear to cause quite a lot of difficulty in self-defence, but there is no reason why this should be so. The secret is to bring as much as possible of the power of the body into play against the weak point of the opponent's grip, usually his thumb. When this is done with success the attacker has no hope of maintaining his grip.

Attack 1

The attacker grips your right wrist with his left hand. As no doubt he intends to use his right fist or arm to attack, your left fist must be maintained in the Basic Posture ready to defend.

Movement 1

Fig. 96

To break the grip on the wrist take your own arm sharply upwards, twisting your wrist as you do so in order to bring as much pressure against the attacker's thumb as possible. The wrist should be taken inwards a little across the body as well as upwards in order to attack the opponent's thumb (Fig. 96). If the grip is broken early continue the upward movement of the right arm, bending it at the elbow and driving the elbow and forearm into the attacker's jaw and face. Resume the Basic Posture.

Movement 2
The grip is broken in exactly the same way as in Movement 1, but this time not until the right arm is taken up to about head height. This time continue the upward movement and then using the liltte finger side of the fist crash the right fist downward in a hammer-fist attack to the top of the head. Resume the Basic Posture.

Movement 3
Attempt to break the grip in exactly the same way as in Movement 1, but this time follow up the breaking of the grip by driving the right knee upwards and forwards into the opponent's middle body. The left knee may be used but most people do not find it as easy to make this movement. Strictly the breaking of the grip and the knee counter-attack should take place at the same time but at first it will be found too difficult to make two movements at the same time. However, synchronise them as soon as possible. Return to the Basic Posture.

Movement 4
Again break the grip with an upward thrust of the right fist but this time take it across the body close to the left shoulder at the same time stepping back with the right foot (Fig. 97). Immediately use the space you have made between you and your opponent to kick forward and upwards to the opponent's groin. Return to the Basic· Posture.

Movement 5
Throw the held right wrist outwards to your right until it is at full stretch and then, without any break in the move, take it downward (Fig. 98). From this position you can kick to the groin (Fig. 98) or make use of the fact that your opponent's head has been drawn forward

Fig. 97

Fig. 98

to drive the left knee upwards into his face (Fig. 99).
The left knee has to be used,
as by taking the right arm
outwards you tend to place
your weight on the right
foot. Now return to the
Basic Posture.

Fig. 99

Note: Throughout the movements and counters I have
made no use of the left
arm. I have already pointed
out that it is held back to
ward-off any attack to your
body which the opponent
may make as a follow-up
to the grip on the wrist, but
it must not be completely
overlooked. It should be used to punch to the opponent's
body as the opportunity arises.

Attack 2
Again your right wrist is gripped but this time by your
opponent's right hand. This is not such a dangerous
attack as the opponent is out to your right and is not in
such a good position to follow up with an attack to your
body. The main dangers are left-hand punches to your
head or right side.

Movement 1
Fling your right arm outwards and upwards to about
shoulder level thus putting the weight and strength of
the arm against the opponent's thumb. Immediately it is
free turn the right wrist clockwise and deliver a cut to the
side or front of the opponent's neck with the little finger
edge of the right hand. Alternatively a hammer-fist attack
can be made to the opponent's left temple. Return to
the Basic Posture.

Movement 2

Thrust the right arm a little outwards and downwards. Carry it straight down until it is slightly behind you. This doubles the opponent up leaving him open to an upward blow to the right side of the head with the left knee (Fig. 100). Return to the Basic Posture.

Fig. 100

Movement 3

Thrust your held right arm upwards and across your body aiming at your left shoulder or higher. This brings your opponent to your left and straightens his body as you thrust upwards. As he straightens drive your left fist into his middle body or, if this is not in effective range, into his right side. Return to the Basic Posture.

Attack 3

Your left wrist is held by your opponent's right hand.

Movement 1

Take your left wrist and arm sharply upwards twisting it as you do so to increase the pressure on the thumb. At the same time the wrist should be taken inward across your body a little. If the grip is broken early continue the upward movement of the left arm, bending it at the elbow and driving the elbow and forearm to the attacker's jaw and face. Resume the Basic Posture.

Movement 2

Break the grip exactly as described in Movement 1 but this time you do not succeed in freeing your left wrist until it has been taken up to above head height. Take the opportunity to carry the left arm high enough to enable you to turn the arm so that you can deliver a left-hand cut to the neck or a hammer-fist blow to the side of the head. In the latter case the little finger edge of the fist is used and in the former the little finger edge of the hand. Return to the Basic Posture.

Movement 3

Attempt to break the grip in exactly the same way as in Movement 1 but this time follow up the breaking of the grip by driving the left knee upwards and forwards into the opponent's middle body. The right knee may be used but most people do not find it as easy as using the left. As soon as you become familiar with the movement, counter-attack with the knee at the same time that you break the grip. Resume the Basic Posture.

Movement 4

Again break the grip with an upward thrust of the left fist, taking it close to the right shoulder and at the same time stepping back with the left foot. Immediately use the space so provided to kick forward and upwards to the opponent's groin with the left foot. Return to the Basic Posture.

Movement 5

Throw the left wrist outwards to your left until the arm is at full stretch and then without any break in the movement take it downward. This downward thrust is intended to lean the opponent forward, which enables you to drive

your right knee upward to his face. You are unable to use
the left knee as the movement of the left arm as you
break the grip upon it tends to place your weight and
balance on the left foot. Resume the Basic Posture.

Attack 4

The opponent grips your left wrist with his left hand
and in so doing places himself to your left rather than to
your front and is thus in a less dangerous position to you.

Movement 1

Fling your left arm outwards and upwards to about
shoulder level thus thrusting the wrist against his thumb.
Immediately you have freed the wrist turn it anti-clockwise and deliver a cut to the side or front of the opponent's
neck with the little finger edge of the left hand. An
alternative is a hammer-fist blow with the little finger
edge of the left fist to the right temple of the opponent.
Return to the Basic Posture.

Movement 2

Thrust the left arm a little outwards and downwards.
Carry it straight down until it is a little to the rear of
your left side. This rearward movement bends the
opponent forward, leaving him open to an upward blow
to the left side of his head with the right knee. Resume
the Basic Posture.

Movement 3

Thrust your left arm, which is being held, upwards and
across your body in the direction of your right shoulder
and higher. This draws your opponent to your right and
straightens his body as you thrust upwards and exposes
his middle body to attack. At once take this opportunity
to drive your right fist into the middle of his body. It is
possible that this target may be out of range. If so punch
with your right fist into his left side. Return to the Basic
Posture.

Attack 5

The attacker uses both hands to grip your left wrist. This grip can be broken as will be described in Movement 1 but it is doubtful whether the effort is worth while especially as it may develop into a battle of strength. It is probably better to use the held arm to pull or push the opponent into position for an attack with the free arm or the legs.

Note: If you push against the attacker's arm or arms when they are pointing straight at you they are very strong. On the other hand if you push them sideways no great strength is required to move them (Fig. 101).

Fig. 101   Fig. 102

When you re-read the attacks and methods of defeating the opponent's grips already described in this chapter you will appreciate that these are the methods applied. The use of correct principle is even more important when the opponent develops greater strength against you at any one particular point as he does by holding one of your arms with both hands.

Movement 1

Ignore the grip on the wrist completely and stiffening the fingers of the right hand, which should be outstretched, drive the fingertips upwards into the opponent's throat. Resume the Basic Posture.

Movement 2

Again ignore the grip and strike upwards with the stiffened outstretched fingers of the right hand but this time spread the fingers so that there is a "V" with the little and adjoining finger on one side and the other three on the other (Fig. 102). This time the target is the opponent's eyes. Return to the Basic Posture.

Movement 3

Swing the held left arm to your left without bending it. This takes both his hands away from the front of his body. Take advantage of this to drive your right knee

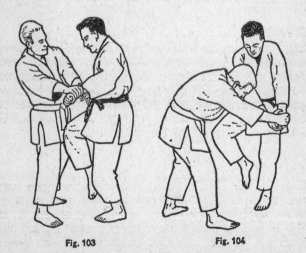

Fig. 103   Fig. 104

forward and upward into his groin (Fig. 103). The outward swing to the left of the left arm is not very difficult despite the two-hand hold on it as the arm is taken sideways, thus moving the opponent's arms in the direction in which they are weak. At the end of the movement resume the Basic Posture.

Movement 4

Swing the held left arm outwards to your left and a little to your rear, at the same time stepping back with your left foot. Immediately use your right foot to kick to the opponent's groin or stomach. The left arm is taken a little to the left rear to avoid it being left behind as you withdraw the left foot. Resume the Basic Posture.

Movement 5

Drive the left hand, which is being held straight downwards, towards the ground so drawing the opponent's head and upper body forward. As this occurs drive the right knee upwards and forwards to the opponent's face. Move back into the Basic Posture.

Movement 6

Clasp your held left hand with your right, thus bringing the strength of both arms into action. At once drive straight downwards and to your left side to bend the attacker forward and counter by driving the right knee upwards into his left side (Fig. 104). You may not be able to attack to his face as your right arm may well be in the way. Return to the Basic Posture.

Movement 7

Clasp the held left hand with your right and drive both arms upwards and backwards to your own chest or higher, stepping back with your left foot as you do so (Fig. 105). This should break the opponent's grasp and enable you to turn your right hand and deliver a downward cut to the neck with the little finger edge of your right hand. An alternative is a hammer-fist blow to the head or left temple with the little finger side of your clenched right fist. Return to the Basic Posture.

Fig. 105

Movement 8

Again clasp the held left hand with the right and drive upwards and backwards, stepping back with the left foot as you do so. As soon as the balance is transferred to the left foot withdraw the right hip and leg and kick forwards and upwards to the opponent's groin. Resume the Basic Posture.

Movement 9

This counter commences in exactly the same way as Movement 8 but you do not step back with the left foot. This leaves you too close to the opponent to kick so instead the right knee is driven upwards and forwards into the opponent's groin. The Basic Posture is resumed.

Note: In the above movements where the arms are thrust upwards to break the grip there is no reason why the counter should be made with the right hand or foot. The left would be equally effective. I have described the right as most readers will be right handed and this will be the movement which comes most easily to them. Where the defence commences by thrusting the arms to the left or right the counter-attack must be made with the leg described as the other will not be able to reach the target.

Attack 6

The attacker uses both hands to grip your right wrist. This hold is usually too strong to break with the arm which is held alone but the opponent's arms can be swung sideways or upwards by correct movement of the one arm alone.

Movement 1

Ignore the grip on the wrist completely and extending the fingers of the free left hand stiffen them and thrust them forwards and upwards into the opponent's throat. Take your hands back into the Basic Posture.

Movement 2

Again ignore the grip and spreading out the fingers of the left hand into a "V" stiffen them and thrust the fingertips forwards and upwards into the attacker's eyes. Back to the Basic Posture.

Movement 3

Swing the held arm to your right. This takes both his hands away from the front of his body. Immediately take advantage of this opening to drive your left knee forward and upward into his groin. The swing of the arm which is held by both the opponent's hands is not difficult as it moves them sideways but the movement should be powerful and sudden. Return to the Basic Posture.

Movement 4

Swing the held right arm outwards to your right and a little to your rear, at the same time stepping back with your right foot. Immediately use your left foot to kick to the opponent's groin or stomach. Basic Posture again.

Movement 5

Drive the right hand, which is being held, straight downwards towards the ground so driving the opponent's head and upper body forward. As this occurs drive the left knee upwards and forwards to the opponent's face. Return to the Basic Posture.

Movement 6

Clasp your held right hand with your left thus bringing the strength of both arms into action. At once drive straight downwards to bend the attacker forward and counter by driving the left knee upwards into his right side.

As a rule the knee cannot be driven to the head as your left arm is likely to be in the way. Return to the Basic Posture.

Movement 7

Clasp the held right hand with your left and drive both arms upwards and backwards to your own chest or higher, stepping back with your right foot as you do so. This should break the opponent's grasp and enable you to turn your left hand and deliver a downward cut to the neck with the little finger edge of your left hand. An alternative is a hammer-fist blow to the head or temple with the little finger side of your clenched left fist. Return to the Basic Posture.

Movement 8

Clasp the held right hand with the left and drive upwards and backwards, stepping back with the right foot as you do so. As soon as the balance is transferred to the right foot withdraw the left hip and leg and kick forwards and upwards to the opponent's groin. Return to the Basic Posture.

Movement 9

The counter commences in exactly the same manner as Movement 8 but this time do not step back with the right foot. As you are too close to the opponent to kick, drive the left knee forwards and upwards to the opponent's groin. Resume the Basic Posture.

Attack 7

This time your opponent faces you, gripping both your wrists. That is to say he holds your left wrist with his right hand and your right with his left hand (Fig. 106).

Fig. 106   Fig. 107

Movement 1

Working against the weak points of his grip swing your arms outwards and upwards in a circular movement, clenching your fists as you do so to provide additional power (Fig. 107). This movement tends to straighten his body. Immediately take advantage of this to drive either knee to his groin or stomach.

Movement 2

Clench your fists and swing your arms in a circular movement outwards and backwards, stepping back with the left foot as you do so (Fig. 108). This movement draws the attacker's head downwards so that the right knee can be driven upwards into his face. Resume the Basic Posture.

Movement 3

Exactly as Movement 2 except that you step back with the right foot and use the left knee for the counter-attack to the face.

Fig. 108

Movement 4

Swing the arms outwards and upwards, stepping back with the left foot as you do so. By stepping back you provide a space between yourself and the opponent. Use this to kick forward and upward to the opponent's groin with the right foot. Return to the Basic Posture.

Movement 5

Identical to Movement 4 except you step back with the right foot and make the kick with the left.

Note: When you swing your arms sideways the main object is to attack your opponent's arms where they are weakest. That is to the side, thus making his body defenceless against your knee or kick counter-attack. It is likely, however, that a powerful and sudden swing of the arms sideways will pull the wrist free of the grip upon it. If this occurs there are other counters which can be made, this time with the hands and fists.

Movement 6

Swing the arms sideways and upwards in a circular movement. As you do so, you manage to free your right wrist from the grip upon it. Continue the upward movement of the arm until it is above shoulder height, then straightening the fingers and turning the forearm clockwise deliver a downward cut to the side of his neck with the little finger edge of the hand. As an alternative you can keep the fist clenched and deliver a hammer-fist blow with the little finger side of the fist to the opponent's left temple or left side of his head. Return to the Basic Posture.

Movement 7

Do as for Movement 6 except that it is the left arm which is freed and delivers the cut to the neck or the hammer-fist blow to the head. This time the forearm has to be turned anti-clockwise.

Movement 8

Take the arms backwards and outwards, stepping back with the right foot as you do so. To free the right arm turn the right wrist violently clockwise towards the end of its backward and outward movement. As the wrist is freed step in again with the right foot, driving your right fist to the opponent's middle body or head. Alternatively, the fingers of the right hand can be straightened and the fingertips driven to his throat or head. Return to the Basic Posture.

Movement 9

As Movement 8 except that you step back with the left foot, attempting to free the left wrist by rotating it strongly anti-clockwise. As the wrist is freed step in again with the left foot, driving the left fist to the opponent's middle body or head. Alternatively, straighten the fingers of the left hand and drive them to the opponent's throat or head. Now return to the Basic Posture.

21. Breaking Grips upon the Neck

WHEN neck locks, which include locks which strangle and choke, are taught to judo beginners it is always noticeable to me how quickly even a little pressure on the neck brings about a submission. In fact not only does a submission come at once but the pressure results in what is only a little less than a panic. However, in a very short time these judo beginners realise how much the dangers of such locks are over-rated and use the time which is almost always available to take the appropriate counter-measures.

I do not want to give the impression that no danger results from an attempt to strangle you, it most certainly does, but rather to point out that panic can do no more than help the attacker.

Somehow the natural reaction, which is to grip the attacker's hands, and tear them away, must be resisted and instead counter-measures which have a good chance of success must be taken.

Attack 1

The opponent facing you grips your throat with both hands. His thumbs are in the middle of your throat with fingers at the sides of your neck.

Note: A little experiment will show that to exert any pressure on your neck the attacker must bend his arms at the elbows. If he keeps his arms straight he cannot press hard. By having to bend his arms he brings himself within range of your straight arm, thus presenting an opportunity for a counter-attack. Similarly, if you just move back away from him, he cannot exert sufficient pressure.

Obviously danger arises here of being pushed back against a solid object such as a wall or of falling.

Movement 1

Take advantage of the attacker's bent arms as he attempts to choke you to straighten the fingers of your right hand (or left) and drive them forwards and upwards into his throat. Return to the Basic Posture.

Movement 2

At once bring your arms up in front of you, taking your left arm above your opponent's right arm, and bringing

Fig. 109   Fig. 110

your right below your opponent's left arm. Clasp your hands together so that your hands are between your opponent's arms (Fig. 109). Immediately turn a little to the left, taking your left arm down and pushing your right arm upwards. This breaks the grip on the throat. Without any break in your movement, drive your right knee upward and forward to the opponent's groin (Fig. 109). Return to the Basic Posture.

Naturally you can work the other way round, driving your right arm downwards and your left upwards and turning to your right. In this case your position must be reversed and the counter-attack is made with the left knee.

Movement 3

Take your arms upwards outside your opponent's arms and clenching your fists, drive them downwards on to your opponent's elbows (Fig. 110). Immediately drive your knee—either knee—to the attacker's groin.

Movement 4

Again take your arms upwards outside your opponent's arms and clenching your fists, drive them downwards on to the opponent's elbows. At the same time step back with your left foot, bending the body forward at the waist in order to straighten the opponent's arms, thus making them more susceptible to the blow of your fists (Fig. 110). Use the space provided by stepping back, to drive your right fist or foot to the opponent's groin or middle body. Return to the Basic Posture.

There is no reason why you should not step back with the right foot and use the left foot or fist to counter-attack. Should you find yourself too close to your opponent to use your foot, the counter-attack should be made with the knee.

Movement 5

Clasp your hands in front of you, gripping them together tightly and drive them upwards like an arrowhead between the opponent's arms, forcing them apart. This drive upwards straightens his body, leaving him open to a powerful upward thrust with either knee to the groin. More power can be obtained for the upward thrust of the arms if you first bend the knees a little and straighten them as the arms drive upwards. This brings the whole power of the body into play against the opponent's arms. Resume the Basic Posture.

Attack 2

The attacker throws his right arm round your neck from behind you, in an attempt to choke you from the rear, or perhaps with the intention of pulling you backwards.

Movement 1

At once grip his right sleeve with both hands to relax the pressure a little, bending the knees, and turning to the right as you do so. If as you turn you step a little to your

left (that is your original right) with your left foot, you will force the attacker to step to his right, thus opening his body to your counter-attack. Take advantage of this and drive your right knee to the opponent's groin (Fig. 111). Now return to the Basic Posture.

Movement 2

This is a rather more simple movement than Movement 1 because it is not necessary to turn the body so far to the right. Again grip the sleeve to relax the pressure. Bend the knees and turn to the

Fig. 111

right driving the right elbow into the right side of the opponent's body, or into his middle body, should you not have been able to turn sufficiently to reach his side. Resume the Basic Posture.

Movement 3

Again bend the knees and turn right, stepping a little to the original right, as in Fig. 111, as you do so. Immediately you turn, drive your right fist to the opponent's groin, or to his middle body. Return to the Basic Posture.

Attack 3

The opponent throws his left arm round your neck from behind, either as an attempt to strangle you, or with the intention of pulling you backwards.

Movement 1

As usual hold his left sleeve to relax the pressure a little, bending the knees and turning to the left as you do so. As you turn, step a little to your opponent's left with your right foot, in order to draw out the attacker's left foot to his left, thus opening up his body to your counter. Immediately drive your left knee up into the opponent's groin. Then return to the Basic Posture.

Movement 2

Grip his left sleeve with your hands. Bend the knees, turning to your left and driving the left elbow into the left side of the opponent's body, or into the opponent's middle body, should that be within more easy reach. Resume the Basic Posture.

Movement 3

Gripping his left sleeve bend the knees, turning to your left and stepping a little to your opponent's left with your right foot as you do so. Immediately drive your left fist into the opponent's groin or to his middle body. Return to the Basic Posture.

Note: It will be seen that I have advised readers to turn to the right when the opponent's right arm is round the neck from the rear, and to the left when the opponent uses his left arm. This may seem no more than an academic point, but it will be found by experiment that when an opponent throws his right arm round your neck it tends to tighten his grip should you turn to your left and loosen it when you turn right. The opposite applies equally.

22. Karate Exercises for Two People

IN this chapter, the movements already practised are reintroduced as exercises for two people. It must be realised that these are only exercises and under no circumstances should they be turned into any form of free-fighting. They are intended to be combined exercises for two people who are co-operating. Take them very slowly at first and speed up as you become more and more familiar with the movements.

As each participant in these series of Karate exercises becomes attacker and defender in turn, it would be far too confusing to use these terms to describe them. In Judo we use the terms "Tori" for the person making the original attack and "Uke" for the person who makes the initial defence. In Karate we use similar terms. These are "Semete," for the person who makes the initial attack. ("Tori" in Judo) and "Ukete," the original defender (the equivalent to "Uke" in Judo). I shall use these terms throughout.

Remember that Semete, whether he is attacker or defender for the moment, is the originator of the initial attack. He is Semete throughout the movement or series of movements, and cannot change.

It is important that neither the attacks, warding-off movements or counter-attacks actually make contact with the opponent.

The Salutation

All series of movements for two people commence with the ceremonial bow used in Karate. Facing each other, the two participants stand at least six feet apart in the·

Basic Posture and then salute each other by bowing from the waist. As they bow, the hands are allowed to un-clench so that the palms rest on the front of the thighs

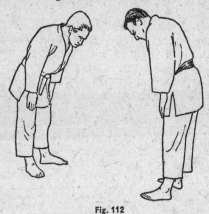

Fig. 112

(Fig. 112). They then resume the Basic Posture ready to commence.

Series 1

Movement 1

Semete moves into the preliminary position, stepping forward with his left foot and moving his left arm forward ready to ward-off a right-hand blow from Ukete. His right hand remains in the basic position on his right hip (Fig. 113).

Movement 2

Semete steps forward with his right foot, aiming a punch with his right fist at the middle of Ukete's body. As he does so, he takes his left fist back to the basic position.

Fig. 113

    Ukete steps back with his right foot and wards-away Semete's blow with a downward and outward sweep of his left hand. The fingers are extended and he makes contact with the little finger edge of his hand.

Movement 3

From the final position in Movement 2, Ukete moves forward on his right foot and counter-attacks by driving his right fist into Semete's stomach. Both resume the Basic Posture about four feet apart.

In these first three movements, you will begin to see and understand the rhythm in the movements of Karate. The attack, ward-off and defence follow each other in quick succession. These series build up attack after attack until you find that the transition from a pre-arranged series of movements to free-fighting comes almost unnoticed.

Series 2

Movement 1

Semete moves as if adopting the preliminary position (Fig. 113), stepping forward with his left foot, but this time drives his left arm into Ukete's stomach. Semete's right fist is at his hip ready to make a second attack.

Movement 2

Ukete wards-off the attack by sweeping outwards and downwards with his right hand, advancing his right foot as he does so.

Movement 3

Ukete advances his left foot and drives his left fist into Semete's middle body, thus delivering a powerful counter-blow. Both resume the Basic Posture.

Series 3

Movement 1

Semete steps forward with his right foot, punching at Ukete's head with his right fist as he does so.

Movement 2

Ukete advances his own left foot, warding-off the blow

with an upward and outward sweep of his left arm. His fingers are extended and he makes contact with Semete's arm with the little finger edge of his hand or forearm.

Movement 3

His opponent's blow successfully blocked, Ukete steps forward with his right foot, driving his right fist into the middle of Semete's body. As he does this, he returns his left fist to its basic position at his left hip. Both exponents now return to the Basic Posture some six feet apart.

Series 4

Movement 1

Semete steps forward with his right foot, driving his right fist to Ukete's head.

Movement 2

Ukete blocks the blow across his body by sweeping it with an upward, outward blow of his right arm. To do this he takes his right fist across his body to the vicinity of his left hip and then, extending his fingers, he sweeps upwards across his body. Contact is made with the little finger edge of his right hand or forearm. As he makes the block, Ukete steps forward and a little to his left with his right foot.

Movement 3

Having blocked the blow, Ukete steps forward with his left foot, driving his left fist into the right side of Semete's body. At the same time he takes his right fist back to its position at his right hip. Both now step back to the Basic Posture ready for the next series.

Series 5

Movement 1

Semete steps forward with his right foot, driving his right fist at Ukete's head or face.

Movement 2

Ukete moves forward on his left foot, sweeping his left arm upwards and outwards to ward-off the blow with the little finger edge of his hand, the fingers of which are extended, or forearm.

Movement 3

The attack blocked, Ukete counter-attacks by stepping forward with his right foot and dashing his right fist into Semete's head or face. As he does so he withdraws his left hand, taking it back to its basic position at his left hip. Both now resume the Basic Posture some four feet apart.

Series 6
Movement 1

This is a left-handed attack. Semete steps forward with his left foot, driving his fist towards Ukete's face or head as he does so.

Movement 2

Ukete advances his own right foot, warding-off the attack with an upwards and outwards sweep of his right arm. He extends his fingers and makes contact with the little finger edge of his hand or forearm.

Movement 3

The blow having been warded-off, Ukete advances his left foot, driving his left fist into the middle of Semete's body. At the same time he withdraws his right fist to its position at his right hip. Both exponents now resume the Basic Posture.

Series 7
Movement 1

Semete steps forward with his left foot, driving his left fist to Ukete's face or head as he does so.

Movement 2

Sweeping his left arm upward and across his body from right to left, Ukete blocks the blow. To do this, he first takes his left fist across his body so that it is close to his right hip, and then, extending his fingers, he sweeps upwards and to his left, making contact with the little finger edge of his left hand or forearm. As he wards-off the blow, he steps forward and a little to the right with his left foot. This places him in position to counter-attack.

Movement 3

The blow blocked, Ukete advances his right foot, driving his right fist into the left side of his opponent's body. Simultaneously he returns his left fist to its basic position at his left hip. The two men now resume the Basic Posture some six feet apart.

Series 8
Movement 1

Advancing his left foot, Semete drives his left fist at Ukete's face or head.

Movement 2

Ukete moves forward with his own right foot, sweeping his right arm upwards and outwards to ward-off the blow with the little finger edge of his hand or forearm, the fingers being extended.

Movement 3

As the attack is blocked, Ukete counter-attacks by stepping forward with his left foot, and dashes his left fist into Semete's head or face. As he does so he takes his right fist back to his right hip. Both resume the Basic Posture.

Note: At this stage it is important to emphasise for a second time the importance of returning one hand to the hip at the Basic Posture as the other arm is used to ward-off a blow or to deliver a counter-attack. These must be simultaneous movements made at equal speed. This adds rhythm and power to the movement. Note also that the foot as it is advanced or taken back should be placed on the ground smoothly and quickly. Under no circumstances should the foot be lifted and then banged down on to the ground, as this prevents any possibility of a smooth, powerful movement. On the other hand if the foot is advanced (or withdrawn) smoothly along the ground, the movement will form part of the sweep or drive of the arm. A little experiment will soon convince you of this.

Series 9

We now come to a series in which Semete and Ukete make a succession of attacks and counter-attacks.

Movement 1

Semete moves forward with his right foot, driving his right fist forward to Ukete's head or face.

Movement 2

Ukete advances his left foot, sweeping his left arm upwards and outwards to his left to ward-off the blow. As he sweeps, he extends his fingers, making contact with the little finger edge of his hand or forearm.

Movement 3

Having blocked the blow, Ukete takes his left fist back to his left hip, and advancing his right foot, he drives his right fist to Semete's head. If he is already close he will not need to advance the foot. This is a matter to be decided at the time.

Movement 4

Semete in his turn blocks Ukete's counter-attack with an upwards and outwards sweep of his own left arm, taking his right fist back to his right hip.

Movement 5

Ukete immediately extends the fingers of his left hand and drives his fingertips forward and upward to Semete's throat. It is worth noting at this stage that as Semete has taken his right fist back to his hip, he now has that arm available to counter the second counter-attack.

Series 10
Movement 1
Semete steps forward with his left foot, aiming a blow to Ukete's face or head with the left fist as he does so.

Movement 2
Ukete advances his right foot, sweeping his right arm upwards and outwards to his right to ward-off the blow with the little finger edge of his right hand or forearm.

Movement 3
Taking his left fist back to his left hip as he does so Semete drives his right fist to Ukete's head, making a second attack. If it is necessary to get closer to Ukete to make the blow effective, Semete will step forward with the right foot as he punches.

Movement 4
Semete blocks Ukete's second attack with an upwards and outwards sweep of his left arm, returning his right fist to his right hip as he does so.

Movement 5
Ukete extends the fingers of his left hand and drives his stiffened fingertips forward and upward to Semete's throat, taking his right fist back to his hip as he does so. Both return to the Basic Posture some six feet apart, ready for the next series.

Series 11
So far in this chapter all the attacks and counters have been punches. In the following series I will be introducing attacks and counter-attacks which involve the use of the knee and foot and cuts with the edge of the hand.

Movement 1
Semete facing Ukete kicks upward and forward to Ukete's groin or middle body with his right foot.

Movement 2

Ukete advances his left foot and, taking his left hand up close to his right shoulder, wards the attack outwards to his left with a downwards and outwards sweep of his left arm, using either a cut or a hammer-fist blow. As he does so he steps forward with his left foot.

Movement 3

Ukete follows up his successful warding-off action by advancing his right foot and driving his right fist into Semete's middle body, at the same time taking his left fist back to his left hip.

Movement 4

Semete sweeps his left arm downwards and outwards, warding-off Ukete's counter-attack.

Movement 5

As he is in a suitable position, Semete makes a new attack, punching with his right fist to Ukete's head and returning his left fist to his left hip.

Movement 6

Ukete blocks the punch to his head with an upwards and outwards sweep of his left arm and drives his right fist, which he has replaced at his hip as he wards-off, into Semete's stomach. Both resume the Basic Posture some six feet apart.

Series 12

Movement 1

Semete facing Ukete kicks upward and forward to Ukete's groin or middle body with his left foot.

Movement 2

Ukete advances his right foot and, taking his right hand

up close to his left shoulder, wards-off the attack outwards to his right with a downwards and outwards sweep of his right arm, using either a cut with the edge of the hand or a hammer-fist blow.

Movement 3

Ukete follows up his ward-off by advancing his left foot and driving his left fist into Semete's middle body, at the same time taking his right fist back to his right hip.

Movement 4

Semete sweeps his right arm downwards and outwards warding-off Ukete's counter-attack. As he does so he returns his own left fist to his left hip.

Movement 5

As both exponents are close to each other, Semete makes a second attack, punching with his left fist to Ukete's head and returning his right fist to his right hip.

Movement 6

Ukete blocks the punch to his head with an upwards and outwards sweep of his right arm and drives his left fist which he has withdrawn to his hip after his warding-off movement into Semete's stomach or middle body. Both move back until a distance of at least six feet separates them, taking up the Basic Posture.

Series 13

Movement 1

Semete steps in with his right foot, punching to Ukete's head or face with his right fist.

Movement 2

Ukete in his turn advances his left foot, warding-off by sweeping upwards and outwards with his left arm, fingers extended, and making contact with the little finger edge of his hand or forearm. Having warded-off, Ukete takes his left fist back to his hip and drives the stiffened fingers of his right hand upwards into his opponent's throat. If he finds it necessary Ukete may advance his right foot but it is not likely that this will be the case.

Movement 3

Semete wards-off the counter-attack by sweeping his left arm upwards and outwards, at the same time withdrawing his right fist to the basic position. Having warded-off the counter, Semete makes a second attack, driving his right knee upwards towards Ukete's groin.

Movement 4

Ukete drives Semete's attacking knee away from its target by thrusting his own left knee inwards and upwards into the outside of Semete's right thigh. Ukete then makes a second counter-attack, driving his own right knee upwards to Semete's groin. There are several alternatives here. Having warded-off the attack with his own left hand or arm Semete could, for example, punch with his right hand to Ukete's groin or drive his left fist into his opponent's right side. Both now resume the Basic Posture about four feet apart.

Series 14

Movement 1

Semete steps in with his left foot, punching to Ukete's head or face with his left fist.

Movement 2

Ukete advances his right foot, warding-off by sweeping upwards and outwards with his right arm, fingers extended, and making contact with the little finger edge of his hand or forearm.

Having warded-off, Ukete takes his right fist back to his hip and drives the stiffened fingers of his left hand upwards into his opponent's throat. If he finds it necessary Ukete may step forward with his left foot, but most likely he will be too close for this to be required.

Movement 3

Semete wards-off the counter-attack by sweeping his right arm upwards and outwards, at the same time withdrawing his left fist to the Basic Position. Having warded-off the counter-attack, Semete makes a second attack, driving his left knee upwards towards Ukete's groin.

Movement 4

Ukete drives Semete's attacking knee away from its target by thrusting his own right knee inwards and upwards into the outside of Semete's left thigh. Ukete then makes a second counter-attack, driving his own left knee upwards to Semete's groin. There are alternatives to this second counter. Naturally, Semete must first ward-off the attack with his right knee, then he can either punch with his left fist to Ukete's groin, or drive his right fist in to his opponent's side. Both resume the Basic Posture at least six feet apart.

Series 15

Movement 1

Semete steps forward with his right foot, raising his right fist and attempting to drive it downwards to the top of Ukete's head. In this form of attack Semete is more likely to be making his attack to the head with a weapon such as a stick.

Movement 2

Ukete sweeps his left arm upwards and outwards to ward-off the attack, stepping forward with his left foot as he does so. He continues the upward movement of his left arm and then turning his forearm anti-clockwise, drives downward to Semete's neck with the little finger edge of his left hand. Ukete could equally well clench his left fist and counter with a hammer-fist blow to his opponent's head or temple.

Movement 3

Semete wards-off the counter-attack by sweeping upwards and outwards with his right hand which in this case he has hardly had time to return to its Basic Position at his right hip. Immediately he makes a second attack, driving with the outstretched fingers of his left hand to Ukete's throat.

Movement 4

Ukete defends against the second attack by sweeping upwards and outwards with his right arm and counters by driving his right knee forwards and upwards into Semete's groin. It is interesting to note that it is very difficult for Ukete to counter with his left knee in this final movement. This is because he has already advanced his left foot in his attack. This also results in his left thigh protecting his groin. However, the fact that Ukete advances his right foot leaves his body open to further attack from Semete's right knee.

Series 16

Movement 1

Semete steps forward with his left foot, raising his left fist and attempting to drive it downwards to the top of Ukete's head. In this form of assault Semete may well be holding a weapon in his left hand as he attacks.

Movement 2

Ukete wards-off the attack with an upwards and outwards sweep of his right arm, using the little finger edge of his hand or forearm, stepping forward with his right foot as he does so. He continues the upward movement of his right arm and then turning the forearm clockwise, drives down to the left side of Semete's neck with the little finger edge of his right hand. Equally effective would be a hammer-fist attack to Semete's head or left temple.

Movement 3

Semete wards-off the counter-attack with an upwards and outwards sweep of his left hand. It is unlikely that he would have had time to return his hand to his hip before having to use it to ward-off the counter-attack. At once he makes a second attack, driving the outstretched fingers of his right hand to Ukete's throat.

Movement 4

Ukete defends against this second attack by sweeping upwards and outwards with his left arm and counters by driving his left knee forward and outward to Semete's groin. It is necessary to use the left knee as Semete's groin is protected from an attack with the right knee by his left thigh, which he advanced when making his initial attack.

Notes: Readers will have noticed that whilst in theory either knee may be used for a counter-attack, very often in practice only one knee can be used because the attacker has automatically protected himself on one side by advancing a leg as he made the attack. This places the thigh in the way of a knee counter on that side. It will also have been noted that it is almost impossible to mount a knee or foot counter-attack with a leg which may have been advanced in an earlier movement. This is because once the leg has been advanced it is almost impossible to develop any power with it. On the other hand the rear leg can be driven forward with the full power of the hip behind it. It is much more difficult to counter a second movement when it is made from the same side. For example a kick with the right foot is warded-off with the left arm and the following left-hand punch is warded-off with the right arm. This is relatively simple and requires no more than quick reaction. If, however, a second movement is made on the same side, successful counters are far more difficult. Should Ukete ward-off a right-hand blow with his left hand and then use that left hand to counter, Semete will find his own ward-off very difficult. A good example is the warding-off of a kick followed by a kick as the counter-attack. Semete attacks with a right-footed kick to Ukete's groin. Ukete wards-off outwards with his left arm and then kicks with his right foot to Semete's groin. In his turn Semete wards-off the counter with his left arm. This is a reasonably easy sequence. Now look at an alternative series. Semete again kicks to Ukete's groin with his right foot, which

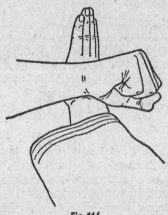

Fig. 114

Ukete wards-off with his left arm, taking his left leg back as he does so. Now he counters by kicking to Semete's groin with his left foot. A little experiment will show you how much more difficult this counter is to avoid.

Another alternative is for Ukete to ward-off Semete's right-foot kick to the groin by sweeping the kick to the right with his right hand and arm, stepping back with his right foot as he does so and holding Semete's leg up for a moment. Now Ukete counters by kicking to Semete's groin with his left foot, making contact with his toes to avoid being blocked by Semete's right thigh. This counter is very difficult to avoid.

You will see that some attacks are very much more difficult to avoid and counter. Only constant practice can give you a chance to make the correct movement at the right time.

Throughout the movements described in this book, I have suggested that the open hand should be used when a sweep of the arm is made to ward-off a blow. Whether the open hand or clenched fist should be used is a matter of opinion. I favour the open hand, making contact with the opponent's arm or leg as you ward-off with the little finger edge of the hand or forearm. This cut with the edge of the hand or forearm can deliver a very painful blow

Fig. 115

to the softer parts of the attacking arm or leg. Stretching out the fingers also lengthens the arm used for the ward-off (Fig. 114), but this lengthening is, I admit, only slight.

The use of the clenched fist (Fig. 115) to ward-off only shortens the defensive weapon by an inch or so and certainly enables you to deliver a very much heavier blow to the attacker's arm or leg. On the other hand should you fail to make contact with the fist and instead ward-off with the forearm, the fact that the fist is clenched tends to weaken the forearm blow. No doubt I favour the open-hand method because I was taught that way. Certainly the more modern technique is to use the clenched fist.

23. Free-Fighting and Practice

FREE-FIGHTING or free-practice must be approached with great caution. The best definition I can give is that free-fighting is a simulated fight in which attack and counter-attack follow each other in quick succession, but in which the punches and other attacks are pulled in that they are aimed to just miss or to land without dangerous force. The contestants are expected to call "Maitta" (I am defeated) in acceptance that an attack would have landed and defeated them in a genuine fight. In contests the referees decide when a blow would have landed.

Before you take part in free-fighting, make sure that you can move freely in all directions, warding-off and attacking as you do so. A typical series of movements is described below. In this book I have described the movements separately, calling them Movement 1, Movement 2 and so on, but remember that all these movements must follow each other freely and continuously without a break. The foot movements are shown in Fig. 109.

Movement 1
Commencing at the Basic Posture (Fig. 116A), step forward with the left foot, warding-off an imaginary attack with the left arm as you do so (Fig. 116B).

Movement 2
Pivot to the left on the left foot, stepping to the new front with the right foot (Fig. 116C). As you do so, take the left fist back to the basic position at the hip, and punch with the right fist.

187

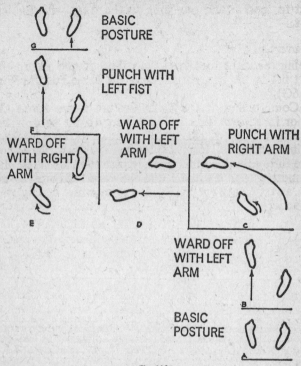

Fig. 116

Movement 3

Step forward with the left foot (Fig. 116D), returning the right fist to the right hip and warding-off for the second time with the left arm.

Movement 4

Pivoting on the left foot, step to the right with the right foot (Fig. 116E), returning the left fist to the hip and warding-off with the right arm.

Movement 5

Advance the left foot (Fig. 116F), returning the right

fist to the hip and punching to the front with the left fist.

Movement 6

Bring the right foot level with the left and return the left fist to the hip, so resuming the Basic Posture (Fig. 116G).

Commencing at the Basic Posture move about the floor in various directions, devising on the spur of the moment series of movements similar to those just described. Include all forms of attack and defence. When you are fully convinced that you are able to move freely and smoothly in all directions and can cope with most forms of attack, you are ready to indulge in free-fighting practice.

Conclusion

The Use of Protective Clothing

HERE again we have a very great difference of opinion. These opinions vary from those who wear no protective clothing to others who protect their bodies to the extent that they wear an outfit very similar to that of the ice hockey player.

In free practice it is certainly advisable to wear a "box" to protect the abdomen. This can be obtained from any sports store which sells cricket equipment. I advise the use of shields or guards to protect the arms, legs, knees and elbows when they are sore or bruised as the result of a previous blow. I think that to continue when suffering from bruising without protection is far from being tough—it is downright foolish. I leave the decision to wear or ignore protection to the reader. Certainly very little, if any, protection is worn at the London Karate Kai. No doubt the better the instruction and supervision, the less protection is required.

Karate as a Form of Self-defence

As I hope I have made clear, Karate is a dynamic form of self-defence, but no form of defence, however effective, can guarantee to make you secure against any form of attack. If someone unseen hits you over the head from behind with a bottle, no Karate ability will help you. Similarly to read this book and half-heartedly practise a few movements will not be very helpful. Constant practice is essential. Until each movement can be made by instinct and until the body is sufficiently well balanced and supple to carry out these movements, Karate will be of little value to you.

However, do not allow the large number of movements and series of movements I have described discourage you. Mastery of them all is unnecessary. In fact I have only just scratched the surface of Karate. There are whole series of movements, other forms of defence and counter-attack, and other schools of thought. A selection of a comparative few Karate movements which fit together will see you safely through most forms of attack as effectively as mastery of hundreds of techniques, provided you practice, practice and practice them.

Karate is more than a method of self-defence. It is a wonderful exercise, making the body strong as well as supple. It develops a first-class sense of balance and increases the speed of reaction.

Where to learn Karate

A few years ago Karate was practically unknown in Britain. Recently, however, clubs and schools have sprung up all over the country. Some are first class, but others are little more than money-making attempts. London Karate Kai was formed by Robert Boulton, G. W. Chew and myself in 1964, and is under qualified instruction. The Karate Kai organises regular beginners' classes. It has very little accommodation for spectators but welcomes them by prior arrangement. Information will be sent to anyone making enquiries to

London Karate Kai,
32 St. Oswald's Place, London, S.E.11.
Phone: RELiance 5082

Index